The New York Times

CAREFREE CROSSWORDS
Light and Easy Puzzles

Edited by Will Shortz

ST. MARTIN'S GRIFFIN NEW YORK

THE NEW YORK TIMES CAREFREE CROSSWORDS.

 For information, address St. Martin's Press, 175 Fifth Avenue, New York, N.Y. 10010.

www.stmartins.com

ISBN-13: 978-0-312-36102-0
ISBN-10: 0-312-36102-5

First Edition: September 2006

10 9 8 7 6 5 4 3 2 1

The New York Times

CAREFREE CROSSWORDS

ACROSS

1 Observe Yom Kippur
5 Small snack
9 Foxhole, basically
14 Darth's son
15 Immunity item on "Survivor"
16 ___ Gay (W.W. II plane)
17 God who rode an eight-legged horse
18 Latch (onto)
19 Disastrous
20 "Everything can't work out perfectly"
23 Actress Lupino
24 Binary digit
25 Tactic during police questioning
32 The Amish raise them
33 Figure-skating division
34 Judo setting
36 401(k) alternatives
37 Moves a muscle
38 Word processor command
39 Giants outfielder Mel
40 What a bloodhound tracks
41 Wing, perhaps
42 It's one's word against the other
45 Pound sound
46 Pear-shaped fruit
47 Not continuous
56 Place with a "vacancy" sign
57 Folk singer Guthrie
58 "The Joy of Cooking" author Rombauer
59 Like the Vikings
60 Boxer Max
61 Without ice
62 Hopping mad
63 Part of a venetian blind
64 Othello, e.g.

DOWN

1 Move like lava
2 Carmaker from Bavaria
3 Tattoo artist's "canvas"
4 Causes of stress
5 Whopper rival
6 Just chilling
7 Hammer or hoe
8 "Tickle me" guy
9 Keeps safe
10 "Very soon"
11 The Wizard of Oz's exposer
12 Littleneck, e.g.
13 Robust
21 Part of a sweepstakes's fine print
22 Flies high
25 "Wayne's World" sidekick
26 Speak at length
27 Was decisive
28 Minor nuisances
29 Blessed event
30 Citizen of Muscat
31 Put asphalt on
32 Story of one's life
35 Country singer Ritter
37 Heinlein's genre
38 Laying hold of
40 Frozen dessert brand
41 Where Tibet is
43 Most like a swami
44 Attempt
47 Magazine that had a "UFO Update"
48 Jordan's Queen ___
49 Gillette brand
50 Catches in the act
51 Spoken
52 Small circus performer
53 Square footage
54 Islamic holy man
55 "Six Feet Under" character

by Trip Payne

2

ACROSS

1 Pillow toppers, in hotels
6 Paycheck deduction
10 Place for a firing
14 "Save me ___"
15 Rodin sculpture at the Met
16 Become tiresome
17 Cool cat's acknowledgment
18 Parks of Montgomery
19 Audio equipment brand
20 He was first
23 Acquires
24 Swiss stream
25 Presidential inits. from Missouri
28 Many a car transaction
31 "___ and the King of Siam"
32 Café alternative
33 Children's author Carle
34 Baseball Hall-of-Famer George
35 Over there
36 What 20- and 50-Across did on July 20, 1969
40 Tree with a winged seed
41 Actress Kudrow and others
42 Prefix with trust
43 Early touring car
44 1946 Wimbledon champion Pauline
45 Sign of affection
47 Joanne of "All the King's Men"
48 Spanish bear
49 Female singer at the original Woodstock
50 He was second
56 1974 Peace Nobelist
58 Vex
59 Bee-related
60 Twice tetra-
61 Major paperback publisher
62 Patty Hearst's name in the S.L.A.
63 Many a stadium concession
64 Looked over
65 Organic compounds

DOWN

1 Primary
2 "Woe ___!"
3 Classic soft drink brand
4 Offensive football position
5 State capital originally known as Pig's Eye
6 Works the land
7 Wedding exchange
8 Clickers
9 Imaginary undying flower
10 Olympian Michelle
11 Major New York-to-Tennessee route
12 Bar topic
13 Big D.C. lobby
21 Whiskey grain
22 Sound off, perhaps
26 Bamboo pieces
27 See 57-Down
28 Poster heading
29 Chalk remover
30 Figure on a window shade
31 Desilu co-founder
34 Fenway Park climber
37 Pasta shape
38 Requiem Mass hymn
39 Almond confection
45 Heel
46 Fill with bubbles
49 Many a gourmet coffee
51 One can be shown it
52 Plant with lance-shaped leaves
53 El ___
54 Lockup
55 Genetic strands
56 Weep
57 Excellent service, in 27-Down

by Roy Leban

3

ACROSS

1 Be in harmony
5 Lewis with Lamb Chop
10 ___ out (barely made)
14 Functions
15 Poison
16 Editor's strikeout
17 Removed as with a wave of the hand
19 Altar area
20 Asian New Year's festival
21 Forever and a day
22 Bother
24 Upstream swimmer
26 Chicken of the Sea product
27 Popular sandwich cookie
28 Gung-ho
32 Backward-looking
35 Field of flowers?
37 Jong who wrote "Fear of Flying"
38 Downs' opposite
41 Coach's encouraging words
43 Nicotine's partner
44 R & B singer LaBelle
46 Tough time
48 Santa ___, Calif.
49 Santa ___, Calif.
50 Every one
54 Fly catcher?
56 Baby's noisemaker
58 Robert ___ . . . believe him, or not!
60 Tailless cat
62 Wee bit
63 Savvy about
64 Mom-and-pop event . . . and a hint to the insides of 17- and 41-Across and 11- and 40-Down
67 Blow one's horn
68 Champing at the bit
69 Hankering
70 Alluring
71 Twirls
72 First lady before Mamie

DOWN

1 Precisely
2 "Honest!"
3 Classic Volkswagen
4 Psychic ability, for short
5 Remain in a rut
6 Hydrant attachment
7 Base line on a graph
8 Free (of)
9 All thumbs
10 Mary Tyler Moore co-star
11 Persisted
12 Otherwise
13 Does and bucks
18 Confucian path
23 "I got it!"
25 Mafia
29 Water in the air
30 Foreword
31 Twosomes
33 Major TV maker
34 Boat mover
36 Narcotic
38 It's scanned at checkout: Abbr.
39 Chum
40 Major irritant for American colonists
42 Students
45 Three-part work
47 Tennis umpire's cry
51 Garb
52 Gong sounds
53 Bushes between yards
55 Varieties
57 Tree feller
58 Burglarizes
59 Regarding
60 Visitors to Jesus
61 "___, brother!"
65 Listening-in device
66 Where you may get a soaking

by Lynn Lempel

4

ACROSS

1 Electronic journals
6 Stretchy candy
11 The elder Geo. Bush once headed it
14 Lover boy
15 Trixie's best friend, on TV
16 Some rush-hour periods: Abbr.
17 Pair of socks?
19 Sch. in Troy, N.Y.
20 Comes out on top
21 Funny Conway
22 Called strikes and balls
24 It turns the tide
26 Frog-to-be
28 Spears
31 Architect Jones
32 Stiller's comedy partner
33 Stat for Ali
34 Science class feature
37 Pair of sneakers?
42 Lorne Michaels show, for short
43 Neckline shape
44 Took to the station house
45 Confessed, with "up"
48 Caught, as with a tree limb
50 "March!" opener
52 Time's partner, in brief
53 Means to solving a sudoku puzzle
54 I love, in Mexico
55 "Tosca" number
59 Britney Spears's "___ Slave 4 U"
60 Pair of pants?
64 Engine speed, for short
65 Lustful looker
66 Dutch pottery
67 It's definite
68 Ostentatious
69 Low cards

DOWN

1 Knitted body part
2 Actress Anderson
3 Divine sign
4 Wise up
5 Piglet's mother
6 Gimme putts
7 Homecoming guest
8 Swimming aid
9 Obscenity watcher: Abbr.
10 Violinist Menuhin
11 Fuel-saving strategy
12 Motivate
13 Stage mutter
18 Plains tribe
23 Driver's stat.
25 Pearl Buck heroine
26 Polynesian pendant
27 See 38-Down
28 Bratty types
29 Nasty
30 Charades, e.g.
33 Philosopher Lao-___
35 French gal pal
36 Give a bit
38 ___ and 27-Down (for all time)
39 Comic Foxx
40 Burn the midnight oil, student-style
41 Linen pulp product
46 It ended at 11:00 on 11/11
47 Crispy snacks
48 Beatified mother
49 Dodge model
50 Coquette
51 Get-up-and-go
54 Not many
56 Be a monarch
57 In doubt
58 Backs of boats
61 "Ick!"
62 Andy Capp's wife
63 Banned insecticide

by Lee Glickstein and Nancy Salomon

ACROSS
1 1952 Winter Olympics site
5 Way up?
9 Mexican gelt
14 Religious leader born Giovanni de Medici
15 Hitchhiked, e.g.
16 ___ nous
17 Like morning grass
18 Start of a quip
20 Product at a gas station
21 Puts in firmly
22 Museo holdings
23 Quip, part 2
25 Key of Beethoven's Symphony No. 5
27 More twisted
28 Romantic comedies, e.g.
31 Workplaces with openings, for short?
32 Phoenix team
33 Perils for spelunkers
35 Quip, part 3
38 Warming
39 Take ___ (doze)
42 Suddenly became attentive, with "up"
45 Helpers: Abbr.
46 Symbol of leakiness
47 Rachmaninoff, for one
49 Quip, part 4
50 Fencer's weapon
51 Obsequious sort
55 Dis's partner
56 End of the quip
58 Words of denial
59 Extract, as a chemical from a solution
60 Arab statesman
61 Loads
62 Point on a line
63 Jungle climber
64 Only about 10% of it is visible

DOWN
1 Proverbs
2 Transparent, modern-style
3 Nadir
4 Prefix with acetylene
5 Open dare
6 Ninny
7 Together, on a score
8 Bank stamp abbr.
9 Encage
10 China's Zhou ___
11 Camping fuel
12 One raising one's voice
13 Religious feasts
19 Attribute
21 It touches the River Jordan: Abbr.
24 Do over, as a lawn
26 Waiter's handout
28 Series on a ski slope
29 100-meter dash, e.g.
30 "Shoot!"
33 Pretty marble
34 Spot
36 Bit of fraying
37 Opening of many a speech
40 Pilot
41 Action in a snowball fight
42 Felt
43 Lab glass
44 Binds
46 Upper house member: Abbr.
48 Really irk
49 Military chaplain
52 Map abbr.
53 Circular opening?
54 Primary
57 Stake
58 Catch red-handed

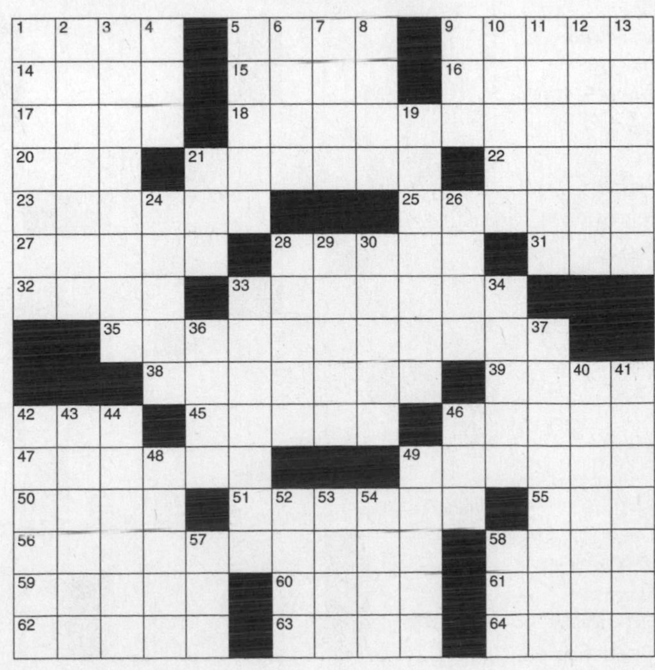

by Michael Shteyman

6

ACROSS
1 Dennis the Menace-type kids
6 Luxuriates
11 "Just ___ thought!"
14 Love to pieces
15 Maine college town
16 Stanley Cup org.
17 Start a negotiation
19 Dover's state: Abbr.
20 Minor setback
21 Raises canines?
23 Body parts with claws
26 Pizzas
28 Mrs. Chaplin
29 Miner's discovery
30 Give a little, take a little
33 Euripides drama
35 "___ a gun!"
36 Late, as a payment
39 Incited
43 Street-smart
45 Spine-tingling
46 Agree
51 SSE's opposite
52 "This won't hurt ___"
53 Seen once in a blue moon
54 Korean soldiers
55 To the point
58 Nick and Nora's dog of story and film
60 ___-tac-toe
61 Shake on it
66 Put into service
67 Jazz great Shaw
68 ___ cum laude
69 Basic version: Abbr.
70 Atwitter, with "up"
71 Fork feature

DOWN
1 "Kapow!"
2 Nutritional inits.
3 "All systems go"
4 Lock of hair
5 Actor Connery
6 Dance energetically
7 Terrier's sound
8 Tap dancing without taps
9 Patella's place
10 Achy
11 "You said a mouthful!"
12 Singer Easton
13 "Amen!"
18 Back of the neck
22 Chewy candy
23 Ceremonial splendor
24 Square footage
25 Ties the knot
27 UFO occupants
30 Angry with
31 "The Ice Storm" director ___ Lee
32 Theater seats
34 ". . . yadda, yadda, yadda"
37 One, in Madrid
38 Petition
40 First 007 film
41 Pigpen cry
42 Front page fill
44 Nay's opposite
46 It has points in Arizona
47 Double-reed woodwind player
48 Chopped into small pieces, as food
49 Not suitable for kids, as a movie
50 Go well together
54 Speeder spotter
56 "Out of Africa" author Dinesen
57 Parched
59 Office worker just for the day
62 Commit perjury
63 Sense of self
64 Raggedy doll
65 Fall behind

by Kendall Twigg

ACROSS
1 Sandal part
6 Hamlet, by nationality
10 Cabbagelike plant
14 Motif
15 Test that's hard to cheat on
16 ___ of Evil
17 Sharon of Israel
18 One of the Spice Girls
19 Emcee
20 Easy-to-manage financial record
23 Early second-century year
24 Writer Fleming
25 Feature of some apartments
34 Flax fabric
35 Homer's hangout on "The Simpsons"
36 Co. with a triangular logo
37 Unwanted spots
38 Got wind of
40 Centers of activity
41 Winter driving hazard
42 ___ Valley, Calif.
43 Where Pago Pago is
44 One who might take bribes for favors
48 O.R. workers
49 Vardalos of "My Big Fat Greek Wedding"
50 Sandra Bullock film of 1998
58 Large diving bird
59 Noted garden site
60 "My Fair Lady" character
61 Allied group
62 It may be put on after a bath
63 Mister, in Madrid
64 Word that may follow the start of 20-, 25-, 44- or 50-Across
65 Speak indistinctly
66 "Yikes!"

DOWN
1 Headliner
2 Drive-___
3 Horse controller
4 Word of agreement
5 It might present you with a big bill
6 ___ bag
7 Territory
8 Bust maker
9 Drew forth
10 V.I.P.
11 Neural transmitter
12 Aid to Santa
13 Superlative ending
21 Annual b-ball shootout
22 Scullers' needs
25 Tartan design
26 Perfume maker Nina ___
27 ___ tube
28 Flying geese formation
29 Paperless communication
30 Negative conjunction
31 Judd who wrote and sang "Change of Heart"
32 Hot drink
33 Cuban boy in 1999–2000 news
38 Beatniks
39 Funny Philips
40 Fond du ___
42 In ___ (together)
43 Blue-eyed cat
45 Hypnotic state
46 Sillier
47 Up to, briefly
50 Sport with horses
51 Corner piece
52 Hero
53 Philippine island
54 "Break ___!"
55 Actress Gershon
56 Shirt label name
57 Mercury and Saturn, but not Uranus
58 J.F.K.'s successor

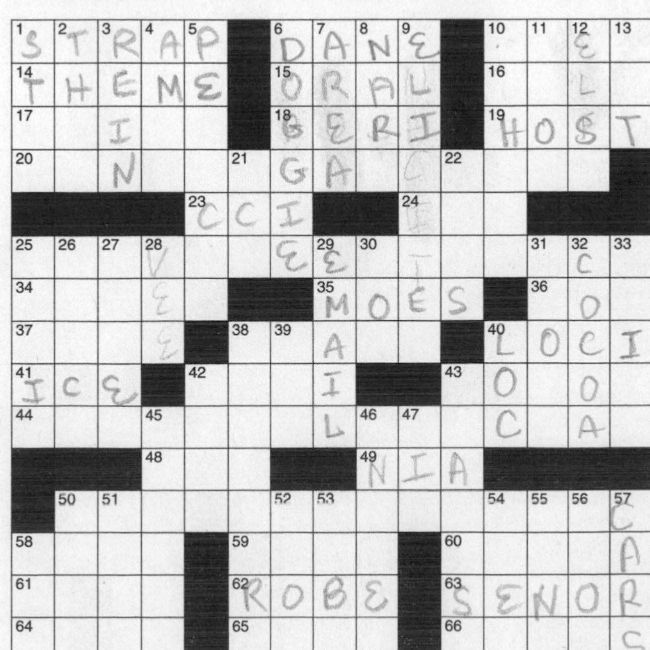

by Nancy Kavanaugh

8

ACROSS

1 Round bullets
6 Dish that may come with a toothpick
9 Helps in crime
14 Columbus's birthplace
15 Ladies' or gents', e.g.
16 Onetime Red head
17 Board that's usually 1⅝" × 3⅝"
19 Punch server
20 Ages and ages
21 Point-and-click item
22 Conflict from 1337–1453
26 Prefix with bar
27 Atlanta-to-St. Pete dir.
28 Russian fighter
29 John and Paul, e.g.: Abbr.
30 Grandly honor
32 Call on
34 Mathematician's response to 17-, 22-, 51- and 58-Across?
41 Desire, with "for"
42 Snack item since 1912
43 ___ glance (quickly)
46 Prefix with school
47 Draft org.
50 Breach
51 Aramis, Athos, D'Artagnan and Porthos, with "the"
55 Grand Prix site
56 High clouds
57 "Don't say ___"
58 Illinois, Indiana, Iowa, Michigan, Michigan State, Minnesota, Northwestern, Ohio State, Penn State, Purdue and Wisconsin
62 Turn aside
63 Any ship
64 It's a snap
65 Trunk
66 Drapers' meas.
67 Place

DOWN

1 ___ Pepper
2 Author Wallace
3 Popular Mattel game
4 Become spoiled
5 Gale on the gridiron
6 Marilyn Monroe, e.g.
7 Punk
8 Rocky point
9 Kind of reaction
10 Rafters
11 Funds
12 Struggle with
13 Speaks scornfully
18 The Blue and the Gray, once
21 Add to the pot
22 Old 45 player
23 Preowned
24 A flat, e.g.
25 Arabian V.I.P.
31 First responders: Abbr.
32 Actor Kilmer
33 Excessively
35 Tack on
36 Social standards
37 "___ et mon droit" (British royal motto)
38 Advocate
39 Approach
40 Trumps
43 "Finally!"
44 "Pinball Wizard" group
45 British knight's protector
47 Sports people in masks
48 Certain Slav
49 "Cathy" and "Luann"
52 Takes home
53 Part of an I.R.S. return: Abbr.
54 Black billiard ball
58 Your, of yore
59 Corn location
60 Airport inits.
61 Silent O.K.

by David Liben-Nowell and Ryan O'Donnell

ACROSS

1 Gentlemen tipped theirs to ladies, once
5 Home improvement pro Bob
9 Boxing ring boundaries
14 1970's tennis champ Nastase
15 Figure skater's jump
16 God, in the Koran
17 F.D.R.'s dog
18 Irritated state
19 "Silly" birds
20 "Do tell!"
23 Sailor's affirmative
24 With competence
25 Greets with gales of laughter
27 Be that as it may
30 Irish accent
31 Hits a golf ball to the side, e.g.
32 Burn on the outside
33 Sunnyside up servings
36 "The Simpsons" storekeeper
37 Roster of enemies
40 Granola bit
41 Four-poster and others
43 Window ledge
44 Hooch
46 How cough syrup is taken
48 Shakespearean verse
49 Barely enough
51 Warrior princess of TV
52 Buffalo's summer hrs.
53 "Do tell!"
58 Snooped, with "around"
60 Gershwin's "___ Plenty o' Nuttin'"
61 Active sort
62 Knocks dead
63 Ball hit out of bounds
64 Top draft level
65 Up to the present
66 Noted Art Deco illustrator
67 Not, in dialect

DOWN

1 Old 45 player
2 "Too bad!"
3 Pinball game ender
4 Seattle football player
5 To a huge degree
6 Slangy no
7 Mariner ___ Ericson
8 Bar in the front of a church
9 Motley, as an army
10 Bullring cheer
11 "Do tell!"
12 High mark with low effort
13 Ghost costume, basically
21 Bring shame to
22 Beer from Golden, Colo.
26 Regret
27 "Moby Dick" captain
28 Yep's opposite
29 "Do tell!"
30 Word before dance or laugh
32 Painting of a fruit bowl, e.g.
34 Long look
35 Leave in, as text
38 Religion of the Koran
39 New York strip alternative
42 ___ Lanka
45 Interminably
47 In the thick of
48 Agree out of court
49 High-I.Q. club
50 Fanzine profilees
51 Strikes through
54 Composer Stravinsky
55 College in New Rochelle, N.Y.
56 ___-do-well
57 Confederate uniform color
59 Hurricane hub

by Harvey Estes

10

ACROSS
1 Nonsensical talk
5 Film repair
11 Lighter brand
14 Quick approval: Abbr.
15 Family support group
16 "___ Beso" (Paul Anka hit)
17 Place for rolls
19 U.S.P.S. delivery
20 Congressional periods
21 Mary Lou of gymnastics
23 Range units: Abbr.
24 Do a pre-op chore
25 Washes with detergent
29 Tranquil state
32 Artery problems
33 Stubble remover
34 "Silent" prez
35 Haloed one, in France
36 Naturally belong
37 Kind of milk
38 Family dog, for short
39 Stiff hairs
40 Model wood
41 Ward denizen
43 Anne who married Henry VIII
44 Socks
45 Part of a jazz combo
46 Summarizes
48 "Watch out now"
53 ___ de toilette
54 Numbskull
56 Hosp. picture
57 Household helper
58 Impulse
59 Choose, with "to"
60 Comedian Russell
61 Faucet brand

DOWN
1 Sails on sloops
2 Memo starter
3 Goes (for)
4 H H H, to Greeks
5 Wooden shoes
6 Floor sketches
7 Girl
8 Octopus's defense
9 Force
10 One matriculating
11 A cowboy might have a big one
12 Middle of a ratio
13 Word that can precede the start of 17- or 54-Across or 11- or 27-Down
18 March of ___
22 When repeated, a reproach
24 "The World of ___ Wong" (1960 movie)
25 Resell illegally
26 Of an arm bone
27 Treat for a trick
28 ___ Jeanne d'Arc
29 Persian Gulf state
30 Part of a simple bouquet
31 Violinist Mischa
33 Marriage and others
36 Literally, "wind and water"
37 Mule of song
39 Noted Warhol subject
40 Pug, e.g.
42 Hearst kidnap grp.
43 Business that makes a lot of dough
45 ___ Hawkins Day
46 San ___, Italy
47 O.K. Corral lawman
48 "Jabberwocky" start
49 Buddy
50 Prefix with nautical
51 Craze
52 Genesis home
55 Facing: Abbr.

by Victor Fleming

ACROSS

1 Stow
5 Door sign at a saloon
10 Mil. training grp.
14 Author Bagnold
15 Ancient assembly area
16 Early Oscar winner Jannings
17 Creation on the sixth day
18 Starchy tubers
19 Title girl of a 1953 million-selling record
20 Pianist who lost her score?
23 Not mad
24 Saucy
25 Cover girl who was replaced?
32 W.W. II service member
35 Dumbbell
36 Turned up
37 Jillions
39 Imparts
42 Computer image
43 Bête ___
45 Prevented from swelling, maybe
47 Collect splinters, so to speak
48 Office worker who lost his cabinet?
52 Pyramid part
53 They're caught in pots
56 Soldier who lost his bed?
63 Busting one's back
64 Salmon River locale
65 Eurasian goat
66 Delivery area
67 Corsica locale: Abbr.
68 "Scream" star Campbell
69 Two slices of a loaf
70 Degree-seekers' hurdles
71 It goes tirelessly

DOWN

1 Galena extract
2 El Misti's range
3 Goddess of the hunt
4 Oscar winner O'Brien
5 Stadium take
6 "Oh, golly!"
7 Name for an average guy?
8 They get the show on the road
9 Dissed, in a way
10 Meltdown sites
11 Present opener?
12 A Turner
13 Kiltie's group
21 Sore, with "off"
22 Cookery's Rombauer
26 Smoke-filled room figure
27 Flowery words
28 Like some booms
29 Test conductors
30 Morales of "La Bamba"
31 Time to give up?
32 Fairy's prop
33 Soothing stuff
34 Salon creation
38 Roasts, really
40 Mid-seventh-century year
41 "Get it?"
44 Zing
46 Köln crowd?
49 Nunavut native
50 Property transferrer
51 Spacey and namesakes
54 Tag
55 Canyon in the comics
56 Knock silly
57 Harrow rival
58 Tough spot
59 Man Ray's genre
60 Punxsutawney name
61 Raises a stink?
62 Marked, in a way

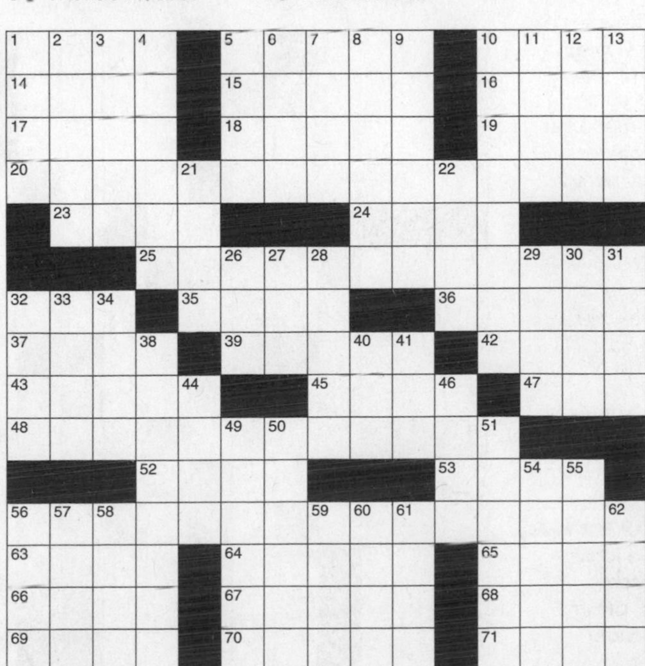

by Kurt Mengel and Jan-Michele Gianette

12

ACROSS

1 Kuwaiti ruler
5 Computer/phone line link
10 The late Peter Jennings's network
13 Tightwad
15 Atop
16 Likewise
17 Not laughing or crying
19 Cut (off)
20 R-rated
21 River's curve
22 Labyrinth
23 Cancún cash
25 Van Gogh subjects
27 Volcanic coating
30 Curtain holder
31 Affirm
32 "Every good boy does fine" and others
38 Doll's cry
39 "Wow!"
40 Diva's solo
41 Best time to act
46 Deli loaves
47 Administered
48 Itsy-bitsy
49 Landmark near the pyramids of Giza
52 Excited, with "up"
54 Gets rid of weeds
55 Sigma's follower
57 Cherished
61 Letters before an alias
62 2003 animated film . . . with a hint to 17-, 32- and 41-Across
64 Sunset hue
65 Singer at Diana's funeral
66 1978 jazz musical
67 Snoop
68 Ehrich ___, Houdini's real name
69 Makes a doily

DOWN

1 Outback birds
2 Item on a hotel pillow
3 "Aha"
4 Chart anew
5 ___ tai (drink)
6 Slender woodwinds
7 Mafia chiefs
8 Shifty
9 Brooks of "The Producers"
10 Oversized reference book
11 Rotgut, e.g.
12 Makes do
14 Cesar ___, classic player of the Joker
18 Boxer Mike
22 Singer Makeba
24 Loathsome
26 M.L.K. Jr., for one
27 Buckshot and such
28 Rice Krispies sound
29 Rope fiber
31 Stick (to)
33 Native New Zealanders
34 Voting "nay"
35 Pilot and flight attendants
36 "___ kleine Nachtmusik"
37 Fill to capacity
42 Rembrandt van ___
43 Fabric
44 Like some Central American pyramids
45 Jittery
49 Opposite of mild, in cheeses
50 Texas Hold 'em, e.g.
51 Intoxicating
52 "Great job!"
53 Krispy Kreme product
56 Voting "nay"
58 Country crooner McEntire
59 Give off
60 John and Jane, in case titles
62 Handful
63 Those with clout

by Lynn Lempel

ACROSS

1 Oktoberfest band instrument
5 Retirement spots?
9 Singer Cline
14 Caspian Sea feeder
15 Saudi Arabia neighbor
16 Toulouse ta-ta
17 Main point
18 Scarlett's home
19 Aerodynamic
20 Drummer Ringo, taking pictures?
23 Off one's feed
24 Jackie's O
25 Rare hit for a slow runner
29 A ton of
31 Family nickname
34 Like "Goosebumps" stories
35 Hostilities ender
36 Spewer of 2002
37 Educator Horace, acting like a barbarian?
40 Renaissance family name
41 Post-it
42 Broadcast
43 L.P.G.A. supporter?
44 Throws in
45 Takes in or out
46 "-ite" compound, often
47 Gardner of film
48 Actor Jack, circling the globe?
55 Obliging spirit
56 A mothball may have one
57 Colorado skiing mecca
59 Playwright Chekhov
60 Weightlifter's count, informally
61 Old Harper's Bazaar illustrator
62 Mango's center
63 Actress Winslet
64 Call for

DOWN

1 Harbor craft
2 "The Haj" author
3 Wild party
4 Deep-voiced, for a woman
5 Bit of skid row litter
6 Letters on screens
7 "Rats!"
8 Fly in the ointment
9 Danish, e.g.
10 Loser to Dwight, twice
11 Amphitheater section
12 Palmist, e.g.
13 Big laugh
21 Drunk as a skunk
22 Seasonal temp position
25 Basic principle
26 Witherspoon of "Legally Blonde"
27 Boiling mad
28 Bench material
29 Dillon and Damon
30 Need Advil, say
31 Pre-fight psych job
32 City or child preceder
33 ___ of time
35 Poke
36 Send out
38 Wound up
39 1980's–90's courtroom drama
44 "What's My Line?" panelist Francis
45 Disinclined
46 Heavenly hunter
47 Take on
48 Exploded, with "off"
49 Savvy about
50 Task
51 Think tank nugget
52 20–20, e.g.
53 Expose
54 Dentist's concern
55 Interstate sign
58 Had an edge

by Randall J. Hartman

14

ACROSS
1 Letter abbr.
5 Floor
10 Part of golf instruction
14 Baseball general manager Epstein
15 Send, as payment
16 Fanny
17 Something to pitch
18 Sister of Thalia
19 Like a shoppe
20 Beard of barley
21 Patient person's tactic
23 Least square
25 Sean of "Lord of the Rings"
26 Bamboozled
27 High-fives
31 Relative of -ian
32 Shirt size: Abbr.
34 Monopolist's portion
35 Diehard
36 Show piece?
40 It's used to walk the dog
41 Red state?
42 Scone's go-with
43 Afore
44 Louisiana Territory explorer
46 Conglomerate
50 Back on the high seas
52 Erode
54 Throw together, as clothes for an outfit
58 Partner of pitch and roll
59 King or Shepard
60 Mother ___
61 Ness, e.g.
62 Michigan college or its town
63 Novelist Zola
64 Singer Paul
65 Site of some lashes
66 In a fog
67 Tops

DOWN
1 Paper-clip, perhaps
2 "My Generation" group
3 With 47-Down, title for this puzzle
4 "As if!"
5 Calculus calculations
6 Has coming
7 Amo, amas, ___
8 Alternative to penne
9 School near Windsor
10 Rum drinks
11 Family tree entry
12 "My secret's out . . ."
13 Prettied oneself
21 Golfing iron
22 Mylanta target
24 You might take a bow for this
28 Goldfinger's torture device
29 Self-proclaimed "Greatest"
30 Connive
33 Dastardly doings
35 "Likewise, for me"
36 Base of a fajita
37 Reading tests
38 401(k) alternative: Abbr.
39 Opposite of o'er
40 Polite agreement
44 King's domain?
45 Whistler, of a sort
47 See 3-Down
48 Library area
49 "Who cares?"
51 Charged
53 Hurt
55 A scout may do a good one
56 1950's TV comedy/drama starring Peggy Wood
57 Home of the Diamondbacks: Abbr.
61 Dr. Frankenstein's workplace

by Kyle Mahowald

ACROSS

1 Frank ___, leader of the Mothers of Invention
6 High Ottoman official
11 Boeing 747, e.g.
14 Hawke of Hollywood
15 Speck in the sea
16 Lode deposit
17 Keep cool
19 Break a Commandment
20 Fraternity hopeful
21 Twisted in pain
23 Gorillas and such
24 "The most trusted name in electronics" sloganeer, once
27 Three: Prefix
28 Conclude negotiations
33 Large feather
37 Knights
38 Unadorned
39 Second chance for viewers
40 Scheduling abbr.
41 Ambulance sound
42 Egg-shaped
43 Smelting waste
44 Rand McNally product
45 Be just what's needed
48 "So there!"
49 11-pointer, in blackjack
50 Slugger Willie
54 Woolen blankets
58 "In" group
60 (The) bug
61 Be a lulu
64 B-ball official
65 Amazed
66 Shady retreat
67 Bumbler
68 Overfull
69 Horses of a certain color

DOWN

1 Zoo equine
2 Consumed eagerly
3 Developmental stage
4 Trajectories
5 Gambler's stake
6 Word with cutie or sweetie
7 ___ Wednesday
8 Whole bunch
9 Cozy spots by the fire
10 Get-up
11 Tease
12 Lake near Niagara Falls
13 Watch over
18 ___ and now
22 Morsel
25 Fairy tale dwelling
26 "Arabian Nights" hero
28 Upper house member: Abbr.
29 Heartbreaking
30 British nobleman
31 Zone
32 Optical device
33 Grad student's mentor
34 Big name in denim
35 Eurasia's ___ Mountains
36 Islamic leader
41 Actor Mineo
43 Doo-wop group that sang in "Grease"
46 In other words
47 Polish Nobelist Walesa
50 Small: Prefix
51 Mideast's Gulf of ___
52 1890's gold rush destination
53 Prophets
54 Place to stick a comb, once
55 Pet's tiny tormentor
56 Back talk
57 Trick-taking game with 32 cards
59 Mad king of the stage
62 Female sheep
63 Newsman Koppel

by Lynn Lempel

16

ACROSS
1 Bit of dandruff
6 Drivers' aids
10 Captain of the Pequod
14 Debussy contemporary Erik
15 Cart part
16 "Damn Yankees" vamp
17 Document shown at border patrol
19 Writer Harte
20 Prefix with duct
21 Yeats or Keats
22 Cape Canaveral event
24 California observatory
26 Salon jobs
27 Fixation indication
31 Meager
33 Served up a whopper
34 Magic org.
35 Feathery scarves
36 Very humble home
38 Score for a 34-Across player
39 Satisfied sighs
40 1952 Hope/Crosby "Road" destination
41 Pool part?
42 Rubbernecker at the Ritz, perhaps
46 Fuss with feathers
47 Zilch
51 Celestial Seasonings alternative
53 Gin flavorer
54 "So there you ___!"
55 Long stretches
56 Part of a suit of armor
59 Derby
60 "I smell ___!"
61 Perfect places
62 Took it on the lam
63 Candied tubers
64 Like Vikings

DOWN
1 Shutterbug's setting
2 Caterpillar, for one
3 Internet commerce
4 Opposite of military: Abbr.
5 Button one's lip
6 Pub
7 Off-ramp
8 Raised railroads
9 Denver is way above it
10 Philatelists' books
11 Interrupts
12 Knighted Guinness
13 The Wife of ___ (Chaucer storyteller)
18 Credit union offering
23 Like the Kalahari
25 Elevator pioneer Elisha
26 Ballerina's bend
28 The King (subject of four "sightings" elsewhere in this puzzle)
29 Cousin of an English horn
30 Catch a few Z's
31 Arty Manhattan district
32 The cellar
35 "Balderdash!"
36 Participate in decision-making
37 Lena of "Chocolat"
38 Sister and wife of Zeus
40 Ran in the wash
41 Settled a score
43 Rubbed out or off
44 Estuaries
45 Labor saver
48 More despicable
49 Steam items
50 Abrupt
51 Lowly laborer
52 Asia's fast-shrinking ___ Sea
53 Ore deposit
57 ___-la-la
58 Words of commitment

by Holden Baker and Nancy Salomon

ACROSS

1 Spur on a climbing iron
5 Temple V.I.P.
10 Less than a one-star movie
14 Saragossa's river
15 Lake Geneva spa
16 Mishmash
17 Macedonian king to those who knew him when
20 Old-fashioned ingredient
21 Medieval merchants' guild
22 Dug up
23 Pitts of old Hollywood
24 Quantity: Abbr.
25 Czar to those who knew him when
33 Waters naturally
34 Summit
35 Bagel filler
36 Herr Bismarck
37 Store away
39 Be ominous
40 "___ the fields we go"
41 It's a long story
42 Fiddle with
43 Prussian king to those who knew him when
47 "Lady" preceder, often
48 Put up
49 Draconian
52 Aplomb
54 Wanted notice: Abbr.
57 Czarina to those who knew her when
60 Mosque V.I.P.
61 Use a soapbox
62 Kill
63 New York's Carnegie ___
64 Whimpered
65 1956 hotspot

DOWN

1 Reverse, e.g.
2 Well
3 Unfettered
4 Sexy lass
5 Go over and over
6 Way of approach
7 Brief lives
8 Stripped
9 Third line on a ballot: Abbr.
10 Kind of shark
11 "The Good Earth" heroine
12 Difficult place to walk
13 Hopalong Cassidy actor
18 "___ life!"
19 Commingle
23 Stoicism founder
24 Yemeni port
25 86 is a high one
26 Gormandizer
27 British chemical lab measurement
28 Like the corn god Yum Kax
29 Prefix with center
30 Minister's calling, with "the"
31 Bulldogger's venue
32 Use with effort
37 1939 co-star of Haley and Bolger
38 86 is a high one
39 Stain
41 Jumping garbage cans on a motorcycle, e.g.
42 Dolts
44 Moolah
45 Narcotic
46 Like some coins and salads
49 Lose traction
50 Far from risqué
51 Enumerator's ending
52 Indiana town where Cole Porter was born
53 Iridescent stone
54 Leigh Hunt's "___ Ben Adhem"
55 Dance exercise
56 German auto pioneer
58 Quaint dance
59 Yellow Pages displays

by Mel Taub

18

ACROSS

1 The "C" of U.S.M.C.
6 Opinion tester
10 "That's enough!"
14 France's Joan ___
15 Samoa's capital
16 Spy Mata ___
17 City chief
18 Lady's escort
20 Bit of encouragement
22 Bent over
25 Frankie of the Four Seasons
26 Stephen King novel
30 Wide shoe width
31 "Farewell"
32 Network from 1995 to 2006
33 Old draft letters
34 Casino supervisor
38 Cambridge sch.
41 Stocking's end
42 "___ hooks" (box warning)
44 CPR giver
47 Antes
50 "Me, too"
52 Pixies
53 Hoodwink
57 On the way
58 Wrinkled citrus fruits
62 Barbara of "I Dream of Jeannie"
63 Cries of surprise
64 Poor
65 Georgia and Lithuania, once: Abbr.
66 Corduroy feature
67 One with a dish towel

DOWN

1 Dot follower
2 Son ___ gun
3 Bit of sunshine
4 Request a hand?
5 Barely gather together, as funds
6 Chinese temple
7 Dentist's request
8 ___ remover
9 Plaster backing
10 Queen of ___, biblical V.I.P.
11 Mexican dish
12 Soothsayer
13 Little finger
19 Impose, as a tax
21 President pro ___
22 Restful resorts
23 Kennedy and Turner
24 "Miss ___ Regrets"
27 Centers of Christmas wrapping paper
28 G.I.'s address
29 M.D.'s associates
35 Skater Midori
36 Wee one
37 Envelop
38 Competition with shot putters and hurdlers
39 As to, in legal memos
40 Use a Frisbee
43 Bee or wasp
44 Catches sight of
45 Piles
46 Rag
47 ___ colada
48 Infectious fly
49 Kind of financing, for short
51 Daybreaks
54 Plenty, to a poet
55 Fed. workplace watchdog
56 Six-stringed instrument
59 Hula hoop?
60 Suffix with chlor- or sulf-
61 Damascus' land: Abbr.

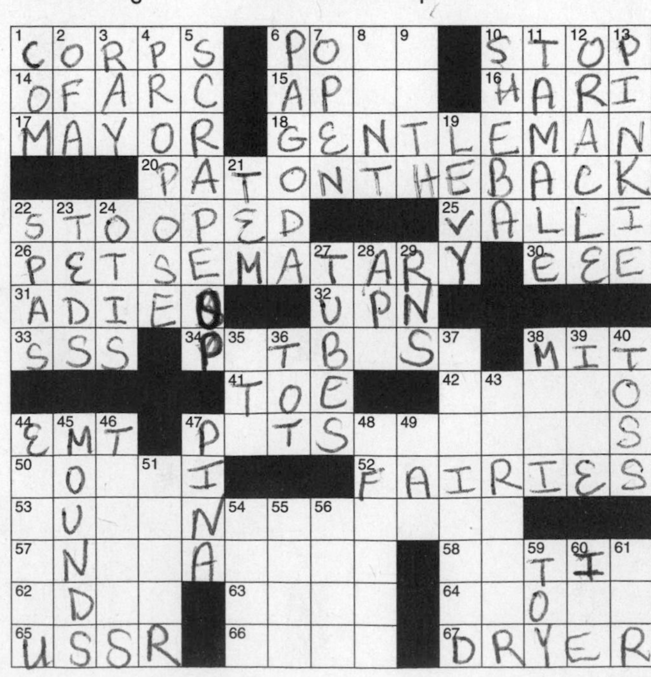

by Sarah Keller

ACROSS

1 Congregation leader
6 Noted movie terrier
10 Excellent, in slang
14 Columnist Goodman
15 Very top
16 Prefix in the airplane industry
17 Large antelope
18 Numbers game
19 A bit blue
20 False rumor about seafood?
23 Needle part
24 Whistle blower
25 "Delta of Venus" author
26 Barnyard sound
29 40¢ per fifth of a mile, in New York City?
32 Greek earth goddess: Var.
35 New Deal program, for short
36 C. S. Lewis's "The Chronicles of ___"
37 It's trapped indoors
38 Finis
40 Polish border river
41 Protozoan
44 Preschooler
46 Guernsey, e.g., in the English Channel
47 Holy chicken?
50 Disco ___, "The Simpsons" character
51 A Perón
52 Timberwolves' org.
53 Onetime United rival
56 Chic scavenger?
60 Usually unopened mail
62 Eisenhower's Korean counterpart
63 George Burns movie
64 St. ___, spring break mecca
65 Evening on Mt. Etna
66 MapQuest offering
67 Parrots
68 Mince words?
69 "Fabulous!"

DOWN

1 Witherspoon of "Vanity Fair"
2 Put to rest, as fears
3 Proclaim loudly
4 Not stay rigid
5 A Gandhi
6 Rest awhile
7 Oil price-setting grp.
8 Lessee
9 Tony Blair, collegiately
10 Catherine who wed Henry VIII
11 Sweat absorbers
12 Parabola, essentially
13 Play (with)
21 Queue cue
22 Kournikova of tennis
27 Sharon of Israel
28 On ___ (how pranks may be done)
29 Spud
30 ___ Domingo
31 C-3PO, e.g., for short
32 Lens
33 Shoot for
34 Immunize
39 Conductor's cue, maybe
42 Shade of red
43 Unfavorable
45 Forbidden: Var.
48 Redeemed, as a check
49 Stubble removers
53 Advice to a base runner before leaving base
54 Penned
55 Viper
57 Iowa college town
58 Actress Garr
59 Mao colleague
60 Bathroom installation
61 Get-up-and-go

by Leonard Williams

20

ACROSS

1 Popular pens
5 No trouble
9 Stopped dead
14 Gray's subj.
15 It may be gray
16 Upscale wheels
17 Split (with)
19 Not straight
20 Old brand advertised by Bucky Beaver
21 Level
23 Devil's take?
24 N.L. cap stitching
25 Showing no pity
29 Minos' land
31 Status ___
32 Actor Morales
34 Investigator, at times
37 Treated roughly
41 Names hidden in 17-, 25-, 51- and 65-Across (twice in the last of these)
44 Primitive fishing tool
45 "Awright!"
46 "Java" blower
47 Public works project
49 Kentucky Derby prize
51 "I can't find a thing to watch!"
56 Cable choice
59 Avian source of red meat
60 Come down hard
61 Radical Hoffman
63 Hawked items
65 Procedure for a burn victim, perhaps
68 Rush-hour subway action
69 Marketing intro?
70 It goes in the middle of the table
71 Deviated, in a way
72 Did too much
73 Breyers rival

DOWN

1 Amount from which to figure sale profit
2 Ham-fisted
3 Procession
4 British gun
5 Put away
6 "Exodus" hero
7 Take care of
8 Late name in Mideast politics
9 Eruptions
10 Emeritus: Abbr.
11 Rust, e.g.
12 Relatives of the Xhosa
13 ___ Park, Colo.
18 Not turning up much
22 Shingle abbr.
26 Suffix with kitchen
27 Labor leader George
28 Can't abide
30 Mideast capital
32 Golfer called "the Big Easy"
33 Tree yield
35 Having four sharps
36 ___ poker (bar game)
38 Pajama part
39 Boot one
40 Summer hrs.
42 Knocked around
43 Send off
48 Telephone trigram
50 Run producer
51 Breezily informative
52 City on the Missouri
53 "One L" author
54 Zest
55 Ticked off
57 Peachy-keen
58 Parisian thinkers?
62 Highlands hillside
64 Party time, maybe
66 ___ du Diable
67 ___ Brooks, 1950's–60's "Meet the Press" moderator

by Alan Arbesfeld

ACROSS

1 N.B.A.'s O'Neal, informally
5 Armada parts
10 Shoots the breeze
14 Andean land
15 1992 and '96 third party candidate
16 Milky white gem
17 A couple of chips in the pot, say
18 Knight in shining ___
19 Waiter's offering
20 California senator
23 Lucy's best friend
26 Water pitcher
27 Singer at Woodstock
31 Pharmacy weights
35 Historical period
36 Comet feature
37 Exactly right
38 Humorist Bennett who co-founded Random House
40 Long-billed marsh bird
42 Abhor
43 One-on-one teachers
45 Pitts of Hollywood
47 "Oh, my!"
48 Johanna ___, author of "Heidi"
49 1972 Olympic swimming sensation
51 60's civil rights org.
53 Came about
54 Comment when things are tough . . . or a title for this puzzle
60 Bulletin board fastener
61 Middle of a sink
62 Baby carriage
66 Tip-off
67 Slugger with 755 home runs
68 Prince Charles's sport
69 ___ and haws
70 Tchaikovsky ballet roles
71 Puppy's cry

DOWN

1 Healthful retreat
2 Rooster's mate
3 Paintings and such
4 Where Montreal is
5 Wrangle
6 Parsley or bay leaf
7 "___ la Douce," 1963 film
8 More in need
9 Old mattress stuffing
10 Sin city of Genesis
11 Pinnacle
12 Cause of distress
13 "Dirty, rotten scoundrel," e.g.
21 Oodles
22 George Eliot's "Adam ___"
23 Kicks out
24 Shredded
25 Robust
28 Mama of the Mamas and the Papas
29 Cousins, e.g.
30 Henry's fair lady
32 Slow symphonic movement
33 Sacred songs
34 "Bless you" preceder
37 Kneehole site
39 Abandons
41 What a golfer might shoot
44 Peel
46 Grp. with F-16's
49 Country singer Tim
50 Ivy League-ish
52 Musical endings
54 Measles symptom
55 Chronicle
56 Lowlife
57 ___ Lee cakes
58 One guarding the steps of the New York Public Library
59 Rustic lodgings
63 Fish-to-be
64 Completely
65 Floor cleaner

by Lynn Lempel

22

ACROSS

1 Cavalier or Impala
6 N.B.A. star in the '96 film "Kazaam"
10 Predicament
14 Eagle's home
15 Hot-and-sour soup ingredient
16 Get misty-eyed
17 Fifth Amendment issue
20 Boat in "Jaws"
21 Guesstimate phrase
22 Church recesses
23 City on the Rhône
25 Gung-ho
26 Ulterior motive
31 To no ___ (fruitlessly)
32 Biblical flood insurance?
33 ___ vu
37 Congressional declaration
38 "Mr. Jock, TV quiz Ph.D., bags few lynx," for example
42 Wrigley Field player
43 Where pants may have a hole
45 Director Howard
46 Lyric poem
48 Australia was the first country to implement it
52 Billiard shots
55 Longtime host of "Scientific American Frontiers"
56 Cover story?
57 Bantu language
59 ___ Toys, maker of the Magic 8-Ball
63 Intelligence endeavor
66 Pirouette points
67 Like most graffiti: Abbr.
68 Flower part
69 "Provided that is the case . . ."
70 Man with a top hat and cane
71 College chief

DOWN

1 Mafia bigwig
2 Frau's partner
3 Rocker Clapton
4 "The Four Seasons" composer
5 Roll-call vote
6 Breastbones
7 Brewer's need
8 A young Michael Jackson had one
9 Quid pro ___
10 Acquired family member
11 Intrinsically
12 Like some cereals
13 Rendezvous
18 Tom or Jerry of "Tom and Jerry"
19 Cowpoke's bud
24 Canine plaint
25 44-Down singer
26 Peddle
27 Pavlov of Pavlov's dogs fame
28 "How ___ you?!"
29 Eric ___, 2004 Dodger All-Star pitcher
30 Blunder
34 E.P.A. concern: Abbr.
35 Unarmed combat
36 Help in a heist
39 Circle segments
40 Neither here ___ there
41 Lake ___, reservoir on the Colorado
44 1962 hit subtitled "That Kiss!"
47 45, e.g.
49 Qatari leader
50 "American Idol" display
51 Fuzzy image
52 Desert bloomers
53 Reserved
54 Tears apart
57 Basketball defense
58 Stratford-___-Avon
60 "Holy cow!"
61 Try to persuade
62 Exclusive
64 Put out, as a base runner
65 Egyptian snake

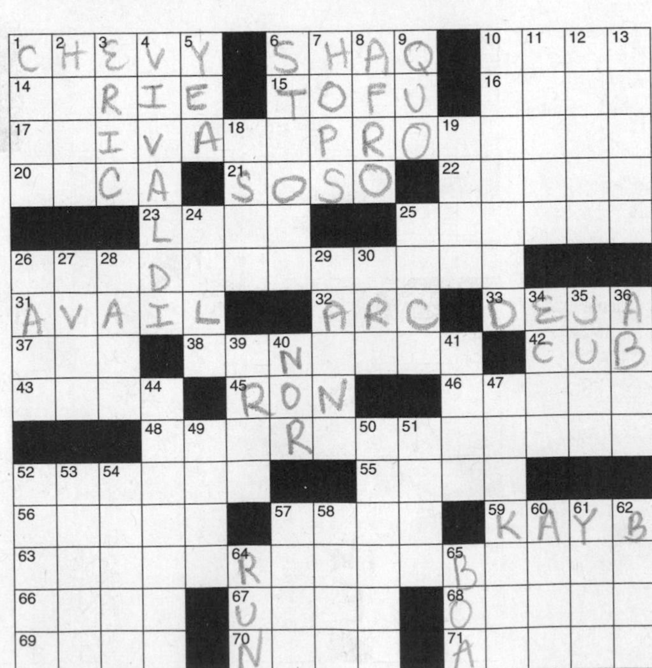

by Barry C. Silk

ACROSS
1 French cherubs
6 Fish often split for cooking
11 Field hospital sight
14 "Beavis and Butt-head" cartoon spin-off
15 Honky-tonk sight
16 Washington's ___ Stadium
17 Bullfight setting
18 Riverbank burrower
19 36-Across craft
20 About 4 million Americans, religiously
23 Elephant's weight, maybe
24 Other, in Madrid
25 Gutter site
28 How the sirens sang, in myth
31 Lobster's cousin
34 Mauna ___
35 Politician's goal
36 19-Across passengers
37 Pop artist whose name is an anagram of 20-Across
41 Low-tech missile
42 Affixes
43 Amniotic ___
44 Fast-paced sport
46 Certain drive-thru requirement
50 Chinese dynasty a thousand years ago
51 Greek cheese
53 Month of l'année
54 Like the most devout churchgoers . . . and another anagram of 20-Across
59 Headhunter's big recruit, for short
61 Not express
62 Allots
63 Hairy hand
64 Tropical palm
65 Spring up
66 Mozart's home: Abbr.
67 Short-fused
68 Deli choices

DOWN
1 Doesn't stay the same
2 Taper
3 "Brighton Rock" novelist
4 Zwei halved
5 Swedish export
6 Poor, as coverage
7 One making references
8 Routines bad to be in
9 "Dedicated to the ___ Love"
10 "Dumb ___" (old comic)
11 Follower of Richard the Lion-Hearted
12 Popular insect repellent
13 Bout stopper, for short
21 ___ Griffith, 1999 W.N.B.A. M.V.P.
22 "What's ___?"
26 Dye holders
27 Masthead contents, briefly
29 Inventor Whitney
30 Demolish
32 50 Cent, e.g.
33 Starters
35 Method: Abbr.
37 Bringer of wine and flowers
38 Post-storm effects
39 Skyscrapers, e.g.
40 N.C. State is in it
41 Bedwear, for short
45 Subject of a guessing game
46 Having fun
47 Carson McCullers's Miss ___ Evans
48 Hardest to find
49 Slams
52 Put into law
55 Bed board
56 Burned up the highway
57 Biblical evictee
58 Days long past
59 Tax pro, for short
60 Water, in the Oise

by Andrea C. Michaels

24

ACROSS

1 British rule in India
4 Eject, as lava
8 Multigenerational tales
13 Cowboy boot feature
15 Read (over)
16 Trashy sort
17 Lowland
18 First-rate
19 With 67-Across, a whisker cutter
20 Dollar amount indicated on 55-Across
23 Sunshine State city
24 "That hurts!"
25 Gathers leaves
28 Mailing label words
33 "Stop yelling ___!"
36 Jazzy Fitzgerald
38 Lend ___ (listen)
39 Niceties following 29-Downs
42 Instant
43 Opposite of "ja"
44 Canadian gas brand
45 "Seriously, don't bother"
47 Mythical being with horns
49 Playing card dot
51 Gives the gas
55 Forms filled out for potential employers
61 Smell
62 Ignoring modern sensibilities, for short
63 Island of Napoleon's exile
64 Hysterical
65 Yards rushed, e.g.
66 "Hold it!"
67 See 19-Across
68 Nozzle site
69 Hwys.

DOWN

1 Replies to an invitation, briefly
2 Separately
3 Minty drink
4 Backup means for gaining entrance
5 Impoverished
6 Sea eagle
7 Full of dandelions, say
8 Summer headwear
9 ___ Sea, which is really a lake
10 Strip in the Mideast
11 Love god
12 Surprisingly lively
14 Letter often accompanying 55-Across
21 Flight board abbr.
22 Call for help
26 North Carolina's ___ University
27 Swings around
29 Helpful step for an employment seeker
30 Preceders of cues, alphabetically
31 Blackens
32 Approximately
33 Memo heading abbr.
34 "Comin' ___ the Rye"
35 Common street name
37 Inter ___
40 Not fall behind
41 Theater intermission
46 Plunge
48 "Is it soup ___?"
50 Luxurious
52 ___-powered
53 Ignored, as a bridge suit
54 Hurdles for H.S. juniors
55 Doorpost
56 Face-to-face exam
57 ___ fide
58 In the thick of
59 Wild about
60 Book auditors, for short

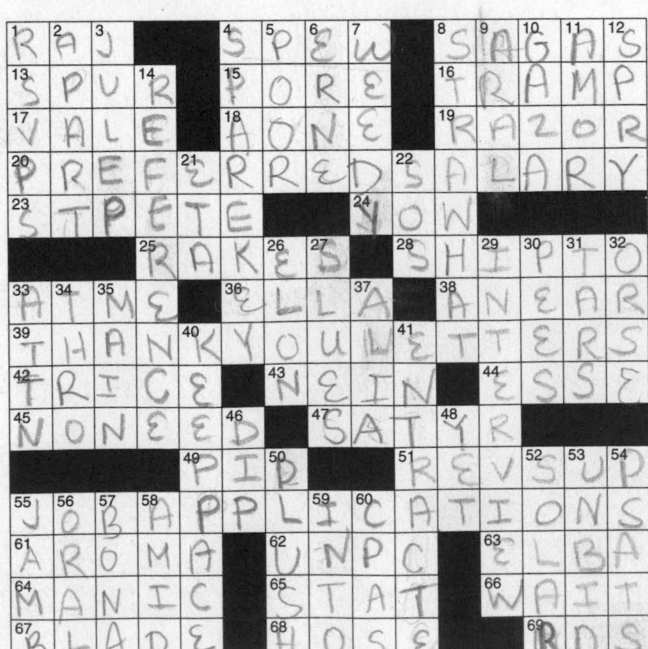

by Michael Shteyman

ACROSS

1 With the bow, in music
5 Dutch pottery city
10 Disney clownfish
14 Satirical Mort
15 Writer Zola
16 Plow team
17 Author Silverstein
18 Like some panels
19 Diamond complement
20 1994 Ethan Hawke movie
23 D.C. baseballer
24 Choler
25 Singers James and Jones
28 Nougat candies introduced in 1922
33 Milo of "Ulysses"
34 Luau strings
35 Run without moving
36 Like tumblers
40 Use an old phone
43 Ram's ma'am
44 Capital at 12,000 feet
48 "Monty Python" birds
52 Gaynor of "South Pacific"
53 Airline's home base
54 Teachers' org.
55 Some e-mailed news reports
60 Leopold's 1920's co-defendant
62 Cook in a wok, perhaps
63 Sweep's schmutz
65 Book after Proverbs: Abbr.
66 Tree with catkins
67 Heavy reading?
68 Siouan speaker
69 Rebellious years, often
70 Snick-or-___

DOWN

1 Chucklehead
2 Cheering section cheers
3 Fastest land animal
4 Spicy stew, or its pot
5 Hanker for
6 Is histrionic
7 Pad producer
8 Spare tire, so to speak
9 Dustin's "Tootsie" co-star
10 Hardly aboveboard
11 Used to be
12 Game pieces
13 Calorie count of some diet drinks
21 Purplish
22 Gumshoe
23 Sgt. or cpl.
26 Shoemaker's tool
27 Chicago-to-Miami dir.
29 Within reach, as a goal
30 Down the ___
31 River to the Volga
32 Tightrope walker's need
37 Stephen of "The Crying Game"
38 Have in hand
39 "Well, ___!"
40 Hoover, e.g.
41 "See ___ care!"
42 Erté forte
45 Seaplane float
46 "Totally cool!"
47 When doubled, sister of Eva
49 Early second-century year
50 Make less dingy
51 Boring tools
56 Aspiring J.D.'s exam
57 Where the Clintons met
58 Fellow, slangily
59 J.F.K. landers, once
60 Late July baby
61 When the Supreme Court reconvenes: Abbr.
64 Ball raiser

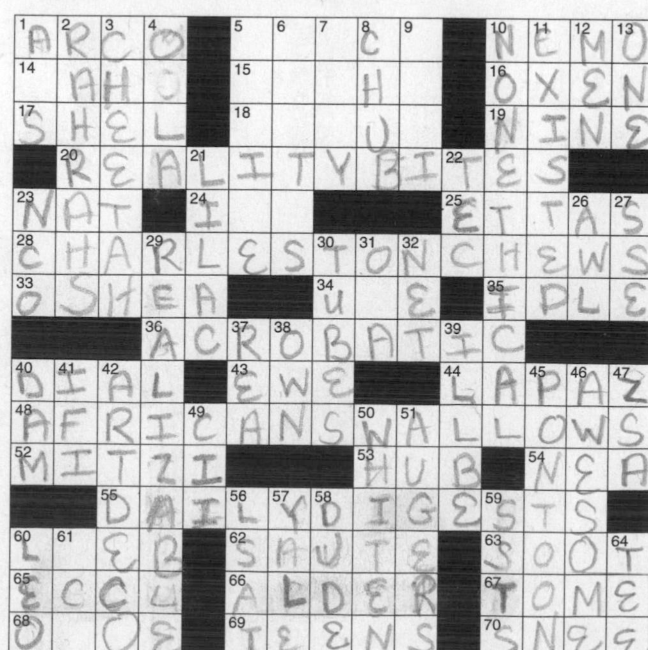

by Stella Daily and Bruce Venzke

26

ACROSS
1 Particular
5 Particular, for short
9 Data processing room
14 Looking up
15 Celestial bear
16 Geneva's river
17 Petri dish filler
18 Wife of Jacob
19 Give the slip to
20 What this puzzle has? (not really)
23 Give ___ to (prompt)
24 Stan who created Spider-Man
25 Thanksgiving side dish
28 In perfect formation
31 Mattress problem
34 Bubbling over
36 Neptune's realm
37 Essayist's alias
38 Like this puzzle? (not really)
42 Without a partner
43 Arthur Godfrey played it
44 Nobelist Bohr
45 A.A.R.P. members
46 Treated with contempt
49 Church ___
50 Liberal arts maj.
51 ___ about
53 What this puzzle is composed of? (not really)
61 Super success
62 Life of Riley
63 Yawn producer
64 Stroke of luck
65 Monopoly stack
66 "The very ___!"
67 Like a celebrity
68 Bronx/thonx rhymer
69 Grown-up eft

DOWN
1 Modern-day theocracy
2 Take-out
3 Biblical twin
4 Loy of filmdom
5 Element in gunpowder
6 Victimizer
7 Actor Morales
8 "High Hopes" lyricist
9 Aspiring doc's program
10 Daphnis's love
11 Boorish sort
12 "Me, myself ___"
13 Bone to pick
21 Stud declaration
22 Twinkle
25 Some two-masters
26 Can't take
27 Is dreamy
29 A tribe of Israel
30 "___-haw!"
31 Built for speed
32 Steward's beat
33 Like a windbag
35 Suffix with duct
37 QB Manning
39 New Mexico's state flower
40 Ref's declaration, for short
41 Provide funds for
46 In cubbyholes
47 Implements of western justice
48 Catch in a net
50 Anti-vampire tool
52 Maid Marian's man
53 Mutt's buddy, in the comics
54 Bruins' sch.
55 Ratty area
56 It's inert
57 Agent Scully
58 Hectored
59 Was in a no-win situation?
60 Candidate's goal

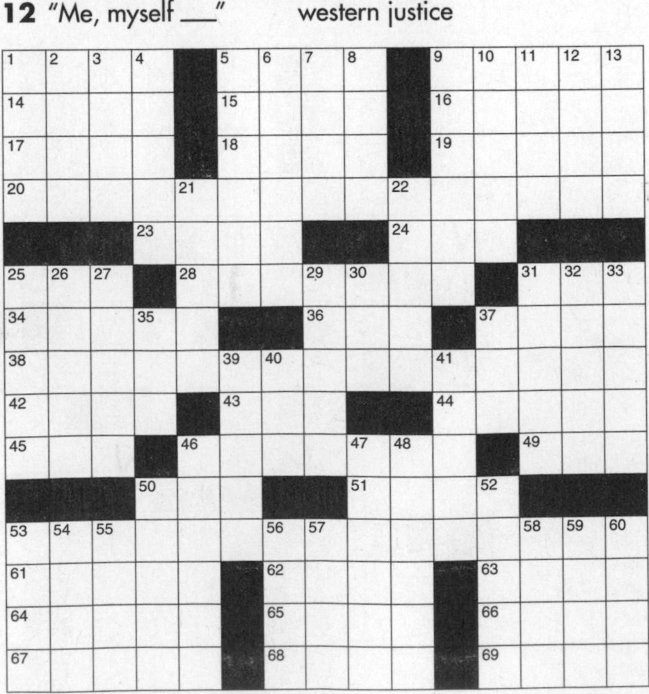

by David Elfman

ACROSS

1 "Whew! The workweek's almost over!"
5 Ready for picking
9 Adjust
14 Indian princess
15 Disney's "___ and the Detectives"
16 Nonsocial type
17 Memo-heading abbr.
18 Alan Alda series
19 Weak and thin, as a voice
20 Chinese main dish
23 Veer sharply
24 Hymn-playing instruments
28 Actress ___ Dawn Chong
29 Slight downturn
31 Trade
32 Wading bird
35 Unyielding
37 Santa ___ winds
38 Reagan's tax policy, to detractors
41 Astern
42 Less polite
43 Emblem on an Indian pole
44 Dire prophecy
46 Frisbee or Slinky
47 Big mfr. of A.T.M.'s
48 Mailing a letter or picking up a quart of milk, e.g.
50 Hype
53 Holler upon walking in the front door
57 State bordering Canada for 45 miles
60 Japanese sashes
61 Wife of Osiris
62 Carries
63 Solomonlike
64 Pics from which to make more pics
65 "You should be embarrassed!"
66 Reply to "Shall we?"
67 Suffix with switch

DOWN

1 Streetcar
2 Los ___, Calif.
3 Like a trailer behind a car
4 ID'd
5 Erase
6 Icon
7 Leaning tower site
8 1-to-12, gradewise
9 Place to exchange vows
10 Events
11 Raggedy ___
12 Bic or Schaefer
13 Attempt
21 Rhetorician
22 Make a surprise visit
25 Expect
26 1930's vice president John ___ Garner
27 Twitch
29 Rather risky
30 Composer Stravinsky
32 Escape, as detection
33 Attempt to get
34 Helicopter feature
35 Make over
36 E-business
39 Surpass
40 Narcotic pain reliever
45 Havoc
47 Squeak and squeal
49 Condemned's neckwear?
50 Raise
51 Doofus
52 Friend in a sombrero
54 Wolf's sound
55 Theater award
56 Bygone U.S. gasoline
57 The "I" in the answer to 1-Across
58 Dumbbell's cry
59 See ___ glance

by Timothy Powell

28

ACROSS
1 Eller of "Oklahoma!," for one
5 Striped swimmer
9 Signs of boredom
14 Dagger of old
15 Folkie Guthrie
16 Cultural values
17 Mouth, slangily
18 Pastry finisher
19 Piece of the action
20 Peace offering #1: "___"
23 Normand of the silents
24 Mini-dog
25 Grounded speedsters
27 Hayworth husband ___ Khan
28 Satisfied sounds
31 Fly catcher
33 Sister
34 Plant firmly
36 Last Olds ever made
38 Peace offering #2: "___"
42 Plumber's gadget
43 Ill-tempered
44 Haifa's land: Abbr.
45 Heed the coxswain
48 Bleat
49 Great Society initiator's inits.
52 Toupees, slangily
54 "Hogwash!"
56 Cathedral topper
58 Peace offering #3: "___"
62 Laces into
63 Have the nerve
64 Trident-shaped letters
65 "Who's there?" reply
66 Blue-pencil
67 Alternative digest magazine
68 Flows slowly
69 Wall Street inits.
70 The "P" of PX

DOWN
1 Inhaler target
2 "Can you believe it?!"
3 Just around the corner
4 Home on the range
5 Can of worms, maybe
6 St. Louis landmark
7 Winter hazard
8 Blue feeling
9 Polite reply from a ranch hand
10 Dumas swordsman
11 "How's tricks?"
12 Like some soda bottles
13 157.5° from N
21 Hoosegow
22 Needle feature
26 ___-cone
29 SHO alternative
30 Do some quilting
32 Ship stabilizer
34 Caribou kin
35 Sot's symptoms, for short
37 ___ of the land
38 Wrap in fiberglass
39 Generous gifts
40 Center of activity
41 Division of history
42 Round Table title
46 Web address ending
47 Like some dummies
49 Deceives
50 Gray matter
51 Trendy travelers
53 Snail mail attachment
55 Apple-polisher
57 Toaster type
59 Fr. holy women
60 "Trinity" author
61 Where to put un chapeau
62 Towel stitching

by Harriet Clifton

ACROSS

1 Ump's call
5 Like some committees
10 White-bearded type
14 Rectangular cereal
15 Papal topper
16 Run perfectly
17 Eastern nurse
18 Overthrow, say
19 Prelude to a solution
20 Marinated dish
22 Gainsays
24 Eleanor's follower as first lady
25 Sing-along, of sorts
26 Group in power
29 Alpaca's relative
30 Banded stone
31 "Yikes!"
32 TV's Arthur
35 20-, 25-, 45- and 50-Across, in a way
39 Suffix with cannon
40 Bowling green, e.g.
41 "Maria ___" (1940's hit)
42 They form bonds
44 Unjust accusation
45 Flower-arranging art
48 Shia, e.g.
49 Some back-and-forth, briefly
50 Variety of pinball
54 Stadium section
55 Baker of song
57 ___ Cooper (popular car)
58 Flock members
59 Clan symbol
60 Compound with a hydroxyl group
61 It's typically thrown eight feet
62 Dodge
63 Like a Playboy Playmate

DOWN

1 "Scram!"
2 Sighed words
3 Cold feet, so to speak
4 Prime bit of trial evidence
5 Drill directive
6 Daggers
7 Mata ___ (spy)
8 ___ y Plata (Montana's motto)
9 Spice in Indian cuisine
10 ___ column
11 Part of a TV transmission
12 Rosetta Stone language
13 Demagnetize, maybe
21 Aden's land
23 Palindromic preposition
25 "Funny Girl" director Garson ___
26 Big Indian
27 "Omigosh!"
28 Be slack-jawed
29 Tobacco units
31 2003 Afghani film that won a Golden Globe for Best Foreign Language Film
32 Uncle Remus title
33 European erupter
34 P.D.Q.
36 Stretch out
37 Source of some brandy
38 Yesteryear
42 Best qualified
43 Eastern "way"
44 Turned into
45 Putzed around
46 Plains Indian
47 All fired up
48 Too full
50 Gyro holder
51 Shortest iron, in golf
52 James ___ Polk
53 Like olives or peanuts
56 Natl. Adoption Mo.

by Anne Garellick

30

ACROSS

1 Top stories of barns
6 With 26-Across, Massachusetts resort area
10 Toot one's horn
14 Onetime Dutch fad item
15 "'Potpourri' for a thousand, ___"
16 Mother of Apollo and Artemis
17 Theater school study
18 ___ Ness monster
19 Natural soother
20 Any of the Stones or the Who, e.g.
23 Multichanneled
25 It may have screwdrivers on it
26 See 6-Across
27 Moving jerkily
31 English cathedral site
32 Bettor's promises, e.g.
34 Cave
36 White-collar crime investigators follow them
40 Patronize, as a restaurant
41 Barbie or Ken
44 Cumberland ___
47 Default modes
50 Vote in favor
51 Start of a cry by Juliet
53 Didn't talk smoothly
55 Sidestroke features
59 Hourglass fill
60 See 2-Down
61 Loathes
64 Look ___ (study)
65 Author Wiesel
66 Les ___-Unis
67 Shells out
68 Indoor arena feature
69 Not saying much

DOWN

1 Inc., abroad
2 With 60-Across, Thornton Wilder play
3 Recurred, as an ailment
4 East ___ (U.N. member since 2002)
5 They may be wide open
6 Tranquility
7 Outfielder Moises
8 Chest muscles, briefly
9 Most damning evidence, maybe
10 "The ___ Witch Project"
11 Tell
12 Lacking a key, in music
13 Is called
21 Keystone ___ (old comedy figure)
22 Spiny plants
23 Physics, for one: Abbr.
24 Overly
28 What "I" and "am" do
29 Niñas: Abbr.
30 Rich dessert
33 Unhappy
35 The "O" in G.O.P.
37 Church organ features
38 Deep-seated
39 Susan Lucci, notably
42 Strong alkaline
43 Batted first, with "off"
44 Grapevine contents
45 Obscure matters
46 Like the tops of dunce caps
48 Prefix with state
49 Fragrant pouch
52 Windows predecessor
54 Play ice hockey
56 Caramel candy brand
57 Sink's alternative
58 Elbow's lower counterpart
62 Aliens, for short
63 Reverse of NNW

by Ethan Cooper

31

ACROSS

1 Big maker of metal products
6 "The Fox and the Grapes" author
11 The "it" in "Step on it!"
14 Imam's declaration
15 Shelley's "Cheers" role
16 Prov. on Niagara Falls
17 Egg-shaped
18 E
20 London's Big ___
21 "Do the Right Thing" pizzeria
23 Actor Bruce
24 Good-for-nothing
26 Some Baltic residents
29 Jazz's Fitzgerald
30 Equals
33 Rodeo rope
34 "Must be something ___"
35 M
42 Massage deeply
43 Hotmail alternative
44 C
50 Classmate
51 Challenged
52 Get an ___ (ace)
53 Prenatal test, for short
55 Halloween wear
57 Morse Tony-winning role
59 Squared
62 Like a game in which batters bat .000
64 6 on a phone
65 Many an ex-dictator
66 Not just fat
67 Elton John, e.g.
68 Flip out
69 Michelins or Pirellis

DOWN

1 "This is ___ for Superman!"
2 Worms or grubs
3 Setting of the movie "Eight Crazy Nights"
4 Stable bit?
5 Drinks stirred in pitchers
6 Title subject of a 1975 Truffaut film
7 $E = mc^2$
8 Mediterranean isl.
9 Yoko ___
10 One of the Ivies
11 Modern means of search
12 "Measure for Measure" villain
13 Minnesota college
19 Place
22 PC key
25 "Get ___ the Church on Time"
27 30-second spot, e.g.
28 Exam with a perfect score of 2400
30 Part of a chorus line?
31 Lizard: Prefix
32 Actress Lotte
36 Auctioneer's shout
37 Italian sports car, briefly
38 ___ avis
39 "Nuts!"
40 Event on the horizon
41 Ages and ages
44 Jerks
45 Sana'a native
46 Yoda, to Luke Skywalker
47 Elton John, e.g.
48 Collected
49 Nonvinyl records, briefly
54 Designer Cassini
56 Granny ___
58 Salt Lake City collegians
60 Prefix with skeleton
61 Darken
63 Formal Japanese wear

by Kevan Choset

32

ACROSS

1 Place to get sober
6 Prekindergartners
10 Repulsive one
14 Walled city in Spain
15 Uprising
16 Within: Prefix
17 Pirate's pal
18 Start to freeze?
19 Nautilus skipper
20 Committee head's timepiece?
23 A.C. measure
26 Prior to, to Prior
27 Ones running through California
28 Trojan hero
30 Tuckered out
32 Ice-cream request?
34 Part of T.G.I.F.: Abbr.
37 Barbra's "A Star Is Born" co-star
38 One way to the www
39 North African port
40 Former J.F.K. lander
41 Spice wagon?
45 Lisa of "The Cosby Show"
46 Gilda of "S.N.L."
47 Phoebe orbits it
50 Champion's award
51 Explosive inits.
52 Gibberish from zoo animals?
56 Where a power play may occur
57 Orbital period
58 Radium discoverer
62 Start of a crystal gazer's statement
63 Library catalog abbr.
64 Passes over
65 Saucy
66 Turn down
67 Dummies

DOWN

1 Rear-end, e.g.
2 Stowe heroine
3 Bomb's opposite
4 A Baldwin
5 Seasoning from the laurel tree
6 Try to locate
7 Sty cry
8 Oz visitor
9 Get starched?
10 Opposite of "At ease!"
11 Actor Patrick
12 Fess up to
13 Some are sliding
21 Guesstimate phrase
22 Porch chair material
23 Pigskin carriers
24 Crocodile ___
25 Dark
29 Loop transports
30 Patton player
31 Game you can't play left-handed
33 Like a white Bengal tiger
34 Battle line
35 "Nevermore" speaker
36 Like neon
39 Moth-eaten
41 Stopper
42 Ticked off
43 60's dance
44 Where Yarmouth is
45 Bailer's need
47 Temporary money
48 Wake up
49 Copier need
50 Singer Simon
53 Big do
54 James of "Thief"
55 Ring contest
59 Free (of)
60 "Am ___ believe . . . ?"
61 Part of a slot-car track

by Randall J. Hartman

ACROSS
1 Top
5 ___ Lingus
8 Sleeping sickness transmitter
14 Film ___ (movie genre)
15 Multiplatinum album with the 2002 hit "Ain't It Funny"
16 Met productions
17 Star of 64-Across
19 Dancer Ginger
20 2004 World Series "curse" beaters
21 Exchange blows
23 Summer drink
24 Henry Ford's son
25 Number of 17-Across in 64-Across
27 Putdown
29 Shakespeare's "___ Like It"
30 Explosive
33 "___, meeny, miney, mo"
35 Sand
38 Catchphrase of 25-Across
43 Out of kilter
44 "___ Lisa"
45 Bread with seeds
46 Paint palette accompanier
50 Artist Bonheur
52 Gadget for 25-Across
55 Check for odors
59 ___ Mahal
60 Part of an interstate
61 Quite the party
62 Small garage capacity
64 Campy 1960's hit sitcom
66 Spin
67 "Xanadu" band, for short
68 "Don't look ___!"
69 Fellow
70 Ex-G.I.'s grp.
71 Gifts at Honolulu International Airport

DOWN
1 Tennis's Agassi
2 Murmured
3 Watches, as a store
4 Wipes clean
5 Comet competitor
6 Nightmarish street, in film
7 Martini & ___ vermouth
8 Hebrew scrolls
9 Like Corvettes and Mustangs
10 Brain scan, for short
11 Money manager
12 Famed New York restaurateur
13 Elizabethan earl
18 Dressed (up)
22 Links org.
25 Rubik who invented Rubik's Cube
26 Bear or Berra
28 180° turn, slangily
30 Bygone carrier
31 "This instant!"
32 Some airplanes
34 "Tasty!"
36 Old-fashioned Christmas trim
37 Summer shirt
39 Ancient Greek instrument
40 Yawn inducer
41 British musician Brian
42 Ropes in
47 Still awake at 1 a.m., say
48 Generous one
49 Darlin'
51 20 Questions category
52 Tempest
53 Vietnam's capital
54 Israeli desert
56 Angered
57 Physicist Enrico
58 Honors in style
61 Pack away
63 Cool dude, in jazz
65 Keebler baker, supposedly

by Roy Leban

34

ACROSS

1 Mongrel dogs
5 Color of honey
10 On the road
14 Meltable food item
15 One of the Flintstones
16 Salad cheese
17 Keyboard key
19 Go smoothly
20 No Mr. Nice Guy
21 Joint with a cap
22 View in northern Italy
23 Cantankerous
25 Throw off track
27 Dates
29 16-Across is preserved in it
32 "Surely you ___!"
35 Geronimo, e.g.
39 Powder holder
40 Que. neighbor
41 Theme of this puzzle
42 Fraction of a joule
43 The year 56
44 Toughen, as glass
45 O.T.B. postings
46 First president to marry while in office
48 Dovetail
50 Memory gaps
54 "Enough!"
58 Clubmates
60 "Quickly!"
62 Imam's faith
63 Door sign
64 Where thunderstorms may occur
66 Teeming
67 Iraq's ___ Triangle
68 Mary Kay rival
69 Manipulative one
70 Bakery supply
71 Make (one's way)

DOWN

1 Hearst magazine, familiarly
2 Gastric woe
3 Played over
4 Most quickly
5 Saddler's tool
6 Do some work on a dairy farm
7 Strawberry ___
8 Toaster, or roaster
9 Autumn toiler
10 Fling
11 Popular
12 On
13 Swerves at sea
18 Cousin of a harp
24 Long (for)
26 Genesis son
28 Board game turn
30 Encyclopedia reader from A to Z, say
31 Caviar, essentially
32 Bump hard
33 It's a sin
34 Painting of flowers, e.g.
36 Barbary beast
37 Secretive sort
38 Lady of Troy
41 Stadium rollout
45 Electrical principle
47 Parade day
49 Make dirty
51 Fresh-mouthed
52 Suffix with Roman
53 Spot for sweaters
55 Oil source
56 Wouldn't stop
57 Touch up
58 Lima's land
59 W.W. II enemy
61 Gives zero stars to
65 Torched

by Barry C. Silk

ACROSS

1 Derby features
6 James who wrote "The Postman Always Rings Twice"
10 Golden Fleece transporter
14 State-named avenues in Washington, essentially
15 Plot part
16 Zig or zag
17 First-stringers
18 Obits, basically
19 A penny is a small one
20 Start of a quizzical Bob Seger lyric
23 "___ chance!"
24 Employed pols
25 Pin holders
27 Hams it up for the camera
29 With 46-Across, song containing the lyric in this puzzle
31 Dowdy one
34 Venomous snake
35 Mark of mediocrity
36 Spy novelist Deighton
37 Lyric, part 2
41 H, to Homer
42 Interject
43 "Scream" director Craven
44 Performed satisfactorily
46 See 29-Across
49 Buttinsky, e.g.
51 Wrap brand
52 Submit to gravity
53 Bawls
57 End of the lyric
61 Race pace
62 Watched warily
63 Good and steamed
64 Clinton's attorney general
65 Stage solo
66 Lorelei, notably
67 Mideast port
68 Plenty
69 Passed out

DOWN

1 Muscles
2 Pi, for one
3 Latin clarifier
4 Soccer superstar
5 California's ___ Valley
6 Cruise ship accommodations
7 Tums' targets
8 Monopoly token
9 Site for brooding
10 Sporty Studebaker
11 Gave up
12 Figure out
13 Load from a lode
21 Go after 13-Down
22 Mauna ___ Observatory
26 Fajita filler
28 Network from 1995 to 2006
29 Shade of blond
30 Student no.
31 Heels alternative
32 Like Lucille Ball
33 Too pink, say
34 Sympathetic sounds
38 Fess (up)
39 Made one
40 Passing thoughts, for short?
45 "I swear!"
47 Be a servant to
48 Neither Rep. nor Dem.
49 Bamboo lovers
50 Teamwork spoiler
52 Yarn unit
54 "Butterfield 8" author
55 Some kind of nut
56 Hägar's dog, in the funnies
58 Shipshape
59 Newbie
60 Feral
61 ___-la-la

by Nancy Salomon

36

ACROSS

1 Swimming units
5 Not tight
10 Possess
14 Geometry calculation
15 City on the Missouri
16 Asia's ___ Sea
17 Laurel or Musial
18 VCR button
19 Pastrami purveyor
20 Actor Quaid transgressed?
23 Giant Hall-of-Famer
26 Not as much
27 Condoleezza Rice's department
28 Bongos
30 Two-striper in the Army: Abbr.
32 Draft org.
33 Frontiersman Boone did some carpentry?
38 Bridge
39 St. Nick
40 Capital on a fjord
44 Actor Hickman showed boredom?
47 Fuel economy stat.
50 Non-earthlings, for short
51 Asinine
52 Move on all fours
54 Hydrofluoric ___
57 Exxon product
58 President Ford stared fiercely?
62 As a czar, he was terrible
63 Home of the University of Maine
64 ___ Romeo (sports car)
68 Olympic sled
69 Assign to, as blame
70 Potting material
71 Popular jeans
72 Fencing weapons
73 Very large

DOWN

1 ___ Cruces, N.M.
2 "But is it ___?"
3 Vegetable that rolls
4 Hourglass contents
5 Greene of "Bonanza"
6 Black cats, to the superstitious
7 Caravan's stop
8 "___ a Lady" (Tom Jones hit)
9 Diner sign
10 Lacked, briefly
11 Sporting venues
12 Gentlemen's gentlemen
13 Omits, in pronunciation
21 Ultimatum ender
22 Man or Wight
23 ___ and ends
24 Links hazard
25 Albacore or yellowfin
29 Intellect
30 Hit with a ticket
31 Thespian production
34 Future D.A.'s exam
35 Ayes' opposite
36 Cape ___, Mass.
37 Low in spirits
41 Hose problem
42 ___ the Hyena
43 Praiseful poems
45 Place to make a wish
46 Assistant
47 Montreal university
48 Advance look, informally
49 It may have a remote-activated door
53 Declines
54 "Home ___," Macaulay Culkin movie
55 Tippy craft
56 Numbered clubs
59 Latest news, slangily
60 Stagehand
61 Sprinter's event
65 Singer Rawls
66 Tiniest amount to care
67 "Cakes and ___" (Maugham novel)

by Holden Baker

ACROSS

1 Mrs. Loopner player
7 Tells a bedtime story
14 Free drinks set-up
16 Mr. Blues player
17 Tickler of the ivories
18 Figured out, as secret writing
19 Show that debuted 10/11/1975, for short
20 Buffet table heater
22 Hail Mary, e.g.
23 King, in Cádiz
24 Bard's nightfall
25 Wearies
28 Syr. neighbor
29 Weekend Update anchor
34 Les États-___
35 Literary piece
36 Wretched
37 Longstanding 19-Across opener
40 Kuwaiti leaders: Var.
41 Take a swing
42 Old Venetian official
43 Announcer for 19-Across
44 Org. for Mariners
45 Lachesis and Clotho, in myth
46 Ground breaker
47 Ottoman ruler
48 University mil. group
52 Terrible trial
54 Network of 19-Across
57 Mistakenly
59 New York's ___ Bridge
61 Samurai tailor player
62 Medal giver
63 Naps, for señores
64 Ms. Conehead player

DOWN

1 Police
2 ___ arms
3 Genuine
4 Old cable TV inits.
5 Nile birds
6 Foul
7 Ms. Roseanne Roseannadanna player
8 Keep an ___ (watch)
9 Dog breeder's assn.
10 Withdraw from, as a case
11 Kind of water
12 Sailing ropes
13 Bookie's figure
15 Hwy.
21 Looked like
23 Tend to, as a barren lawn
25 Kentucky Derby drink
26 True inner self
27 Springboard performer
28 Phrase of commitment
29 Intimidate
30 The best of times
31 Under way
32 Power glitch
33 Actress Sommer and others
35 Surgeon's locales, quickly
36 Dripping
38 To and ___
39 Collar
44 Mr. Escuela player
45 Catlike
46 Big to-do
47 Von Richthofen's title
48 Barbecue fare
49 R.E.M.'s "The ___ Love"
50 Prefix with conference
51 Vineyards of high quality
53 Biblical suffix
54 Benchmark
55 La ___ Tar Pits
56 Foot ailment
58 String after Q
60 Close a show

by Mike Torch

38

ACROSS

1 Fudge maker?
5 Iowa's ___ Society
10 Asian nation suffix
14 A lot?
15 Like early PC graphics
16 Mall aid
17 Start of a quip
20 Big bird
21 Source of iron
22 Pound sound
23 Some are famous
27 Unearthly
30 Elvis trademark
31 Induce rain from
33 Claimer's cry
34 Grant-in-___
36 Milky Way and others
38 City, state, ___
39 Quip, part 2
43 "Yo!"
44 Times to revel, maybe
45 Not the handsomest dog
46 Surface figure
48 Ones who've gone splitsville
50 Circus Maximus attire
54 Vas deferens and others
56 Place for carved initials
58 Top guns
60 Circus Maximus greeting
61 MP3 player maker
62 End of the quip
67 ___ of the earth
68 "You've got mail" hearer
69 Lily family member
70 Four-time Indy winner
71 Rotten
72 Uncool sort

DOWN

1 Boutonnieres' places
2 One found just around the block?
3 Pique
4 Account overseer, for short
5 Car discontinued in 2004
6 Grounds crew
7 "Exodus" hero
8 Bring home
9 Pasty-faced
10 Like hair at salons
11 Gold medal, e.g.
12 Lunched
13 Opposite of paleo-
18 Like some women's jeans
19 ___ time (course slot)
24 Hotfoot it
25 Demeaning one
26 Use wax on
28 Egyptian sacred bird
29 Empath's skill
32 Coffeemaker style
35 Went off the deep end?
37 Sing "K-K-K-Katy," say
39 Big silver exporter
40 Nice things to look at
41 Counter call
42 1974 Marty Feldman comic-horror role
43 Took to the cleaners
47 For no profit
49 Ready for dinner
51 Fountain sound
52 Hold fast
53 Did toe loops, say
55 "Quiet!" locale
57 Part of the mnemonic for EGBDF
59 Started a triathlon
62 Hip-hop "cool"
63 Noted resident of the Dakota
64 Milne marsupial
65 Off one's feed
66 Actor McKellen

by Paul Guttormsson

ACROSS

1 Unravel, as a cord
5 Hand support
9 Fissures
14 Christmas season
15 To be, in Toulon
16 Messages via MSN.com, e.g.
17 "___ small world!"
18 Extended family
19 Backside
20 Old-fashioned
23 Nonverbal O.K.'s
24 Author Harper ___
25 Amer. soldiers
28 Result of a hung jury, maybe
31 Fit ___ fiddle
34 Fess up (to)
36 Driver's lic. and such
37 +
38 Fundamental
42 ___ liquor
43 Two halves
44 "All in the Family" spin-off
45 The whole ball of wax
46 Mt. Rushmore material
49 "Law & Order" fig.
50 Shipwreck signal
51 Instrument hit with a hammer
53 Petty
59 Lethal snake
60 Yankee nickname starting 2004
61 Workbench attachment
63 "Doe, ___, a female . . ."
64 Sagan or Sandburg
65 Glimpse
66 It might be 18 oz. on a cereal box
67 Safe sword
68 ___ the wiser

DOWN

1 Memo letters
2 Justice ___ Bader Ginsburg
3 By the same token
4 Long (for)
5 Ebb
6 "Finally!"
7 Tehran's land
8 What usurers do
9 Gas up again
10 Spitting ___
11 Weapon of 59 Across
12 Wee
13 Underhanded
21 After a fashion, informally
22 Really good time
25 Alpha, beta, ___ . . .
26 Perfect
27 Wee
29 Turn red, as a strawberry
30 Wedding vow
31 Not silently
32 Luxury leather
33 Liability's opposite
35 Cousin ___ of "The Addams Family"
37 School fund-raising grp.
39 Like the Vikings
40 Genetic stuff
41 Change, as the Constitution
46 Fun park car
47 Tune out
48 Walk like a little 'un
50 It fits into a nut
52 First, as a name
53 Lymph bump
54 "Yeah, sure"
55 Open fabric
56 Amount not to care
57 Soybean paste
58 Armchair athlete's channel
59 Pop-top's place
62 Storm's center

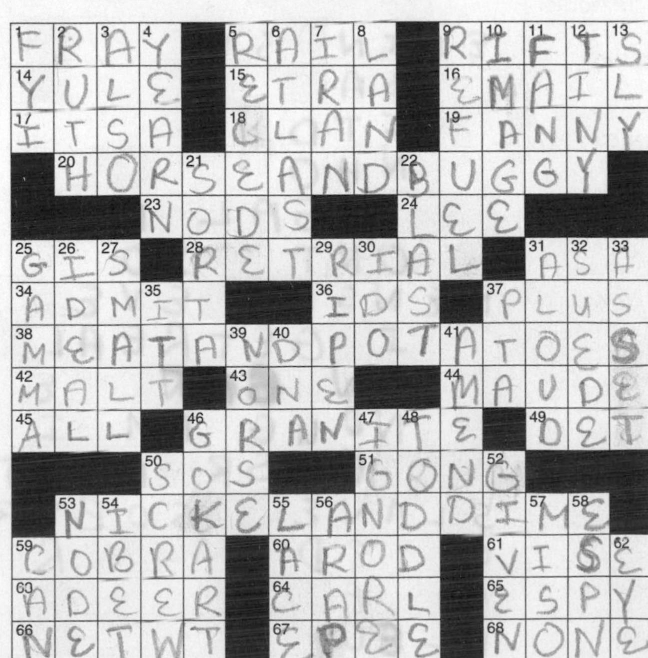

by Gregory E. Paul

40

ACROSS
1 ___ Brockovich, Julia Roberts title role
5 Mex. misses
10 Tom, Dick or Harry
14 1998 N.L. M.V.P. from Chicago
15 Sports hiree
16 Sen. Bayh of Indiana
17 See 35-Across
20 Ladies of Lisbon
21 Crowbar, e.g.
22 "I've Got ___ in Kalamazoo"
23 Soccer ___
25 See 35-Across
30 Geniuses' group
31 12/24 or 12/31
32 Golfer Ballesteros
34 Samuel's teacher
35 This puzzle's theme, succinctly
39 Gen-___ (boomer's kid)
40 Shakespeare's stream
42 Hood's gun
43 Rhône tributary
45 See 35-Across
49 Cold war inits.
50 "___ No Mountain High Enough" (1970 #1 hit)
51 Underground Railroad user
54 Least drunk
58 See 35-Across
61 Follower of inter or et
62 "Marat/Sade" playwright
63 Statement to a judge
64 Chicken cordon ___
65 Cosmetician Lauder
66 Teamster's rig

DOWN
1 A.B.A. members' titles
2 Lecherous sort
3 "Beauty ___ the eye . . ."
4 Famous name in hot dogs
5 Japanese beetle, e.g.
6 Isle ___ National Park
7 Small amounts
8 90° from down: Abbr.
9 Any ship
10 Unbeatable foe
11 Tel ___, Israel
12 Luxuriant locks
13 M.I.T. grad., often
18 Bowser's identification
19 Diva Gluck
23 "Outta my way!"
24 Prime S.S.S. classification
25 Probe, with "into"
26 Bagel choice
27 Major mattress maker
28 Nettled
29 Each's companion
30 "___ culpa"
33 Bard's before
36 Soufflé needs
37 Asian goat
38 Holder of claimed property
41 ___ riche
44 Persian governors
46 Hand-me-down
47 Supposed founder of Taoism
48 Nucleic acid sugar
51 Strike defier
52 Vegetate
53 Gallic girlfriend
54 Fit of pique
55 Creator of Perry and Della
56 Goblet feature
57 Bangkok native
59 Have a tab
60 Jazz's Montgomery

by Jay Leatherman

ACROSS
1 Flipper, e.g.
5 Butting heads
11 W.W. II spy org.
14 Fit to serve
15 Stick together
16 Some drops
17 Spot in the top tier
19 ___ de France
20 Hot spot
21 "Nova" network
22 Not fresh
23 Without support
24 Up to, quickly
26 Rope fiber
27 "Ben-___"
28 When wadis fill
32 Pellets, e.g.
34 Speed (up)
35 Accidental occurrence
36 1941 Cary Grant tearjerker
41 It may have periods
42 Capek play
43 Church part
45 Letterhead feature
50 Burden
51 Hoodwink
52 Poetic contraction
53 Ill-suited
55 Cabinet dept. since 1965
56 Host of an annual convention attended by publishers: Abbr.
58 Hut material
59 Public-house offering
60 Measure of a company's dominance (and a literal hint to 17-, 28-, 36- and 45-Across)
64 Circle meas.
65 Cause of weird weather
66 "The heat ___!"
67 Master hand
68 Lie atop
69 Backpack item, maybe

DOWN
1 Court ploy
2 Struggling, as a pitcher
3 The Velvet Fog
4 He said "Knowledge is power"
5 Retin-A treats it
6 Poodle, perhaps
7 Startled cries
8 With all one's heart
9 Evoking an "eh"
10 Lot sights
11 Rotten to the core
12 Deal with commercially
13 It touches the Gulf of Bothnia
18 Recovered from
23 Brainstormer's cry
24 Haberdashery stock
25 2, to ½
26 Where "besuboru" is played
29 Indo-___ languages
30 He-Man's toon sister
31 Caesar's end?
33 Time to get back to work, maybe
37 Big D.C. lobby
38 One kicking oneself
39 Record collection?
40 1996 Madonna role
44 Tel. no. add-on
45 Black key
46 Eyepiece
47 Got by
48 Pines
49 Spending restraints
54 Like a rare baseball game
56 Part of VISTA: Abbr.
57 Bundle up
58 Oodles
61 Emergency ___
62 Musician Brian
63 Tolkien creature

by Levi Denham

42

ACROSS
1 Wood for Woods
5 Where to set books
10 Community service group
14 Queue
15 Four-bagger
16 Pipe problem
17 Writer Wiesel
18 Breathing
19 Unnerve
20 Hopping mad
23 Mother hog
24 Chafes
25 Tear-jerking sentiment
27 In good spirits
30 Obliterate
32 Wrestling maneuvers
33 Lose-weight-fast plan
37 Antipollution org.
38 About half of crossword clues
39 "Gotcha!"
40 Step just before publishing an article
43 Outranking
45 Sheets, tablecloths, etc.
46 Annual event at 43-Down Stadium
47 Frugality
50 Fed. watchdog since 1971
51 Motorists' org.
52 Change defeat into victory
58 Egyptian pyramids locale
60 Itinerary
61 One with a duster
62 Hawaiian strings
63 Tribal leader
64 Like good wine
65 Urge on
66 Visionaries
67 Prying

DOWN
1 Musical symbol
2 1953 Leslie Caron film
3 The "U" in I.C.U.
4 Visibly embarrassed
5 "Not too ___"
6 The 18 in a round of 18
7 Send out
8 ___ Strauss & Co.
9 Complimentary ticket
10 Santa's little helper
11 Tether
12 Musical instrument for the nonmusical
13 Distorts
21 Owned jointly by you and me
22 Sprint
26 One of the Kennedys
27 Person who's often sent compliments
28 Indian tribe with kachina dolls
29 Spirit
30 W.W. II German general Rommel
31 Sound off
33 Morse ___
34 Denny's alternative
35 Roof overhang
36 Next
38 They may sit in a glass at night
41 He could "float like a butterfly, sting like a bee"
42 Boost
43 See 46-Across
44 Ferry operator
46 Wedding helpers
47 Get ready to run, in baseball
48 Three-line poem
49 Demolishes
50 Bewhiskered swimmer
53 Film part
54 In the raw
55 Shakespearean villain
56 Fizzles out
57 Whirlpool
59 Cigar waste

by Lynn Lempel

43

ACROSS

1 Held a session
4 Crustaceans eaten by whales
9 Arcade flubs
14 Each
15 Kind of ink
16 Former TWA honcho Carl
17 Ill temper
18 2003 Tom Cruise movie, with "The"
20 Children's song refrain
22 Mint or chive
23 Mound dweller
24 In memoriam phrase
28 "¿Quién ___?" ("Who knows?"): Sp.
29 Creamsicle color
33 When doubled, a dance
36 Blue eyes or curly hair, say
39 Like many college dorms, now
40 Lean right, at sea
44 Diva's delivery
45 Copier need
46 "You, there!"
47 Hanker for
50 Greek consonants
52 What Bo-Peep did
58 RR stop
61 Workers' welfare overseer: Abbr.
62 Looie's underling
63 Van Gogh biography
67 Refinable rock
68 Put down
69 Atelier prop
70 Pa. neighbor
71 Alternative to plastic
72 Colorado's ___ Park
73 Otherworldly visitors, for short

DOWN

1 Pitchman's pitch
2 Hilltop home
3 Shoe stiffeners
4 Electrical power unit
5 Genetic letters
6 Cards with photos, for short
7 Certain print, briefly
8 Surgical beam
9 Lumberjack's call
10 Hosp. area
11 Tomb raider of film, ___ Croft
12 Comparison connector
13 Foul mood
19 Cornstarch brand
21 "___ been real!"
25 River of Aragón
26 Eat like a king
27 Snack in a shell
30 Wyle of "ER"
31 Richard of "Chicago"
32 Whirling water
33 Decked out
34 Take on
35 Sales tag words
37 "Am ___ believe . . . ?"
38 Oncle's wife
41 Follow closely
42 Paddler's target
43 NATO headquarters site
48 Housetop laborer
49 Gas brand in Canada
51 ___ Na Na
53 Birdie score, often
54 N.F.L. coach called "Papa Bear"
55 Wear down
56 "Snowy" bird
57 Suffers from sunburn
58 Retaliation for a pinch
59 Hefty horn
60 Quickly, in memos
64 China's Lao-___
65 Adherent's suffix
66 Agent's due

by Kurt Mengel and Jan-Michele Gianette

44

ACROSS

1 Auto parts giant
5 They may be vaulted
10 Sharp or flat, say
13 Does in
14 Timely benefits
15 Cap-___ (from head to foot)
16 Bureaus
19 It may have electroreceptors
20 Dances with chairs
21 Rhinestone feature
22 Gooey stuff
23 Co. that offers I.M.'s
24 It usually starts "How many . . . ?"
31 Puts out of work
32 Like "Green Acres"
33 Bushy 'do
36 Appear
37 Glass ingredient
38 "Dracula" author Stoker
39 Gunpowder, e.g.
40 Navy elite
41 Assault on Troy, e.g.
42 2003 Nicolas Cage film
45 Hood's piece
46 Sr.'s exam
47 Barely enough
50 Liquid-Plumr competitor
53 Red-white-and-blue inits.
56 Their initials can be found consecutively in 16-, 24- and 42-Across
59 Diner sign
60 1978 Peace Nobelist
61 Some mayhem
62 Common title
63 It may be skipped
64 Fair

DOWN

1 "Good one!"
2 Have a hankering
3 Floor it, with "out"
4 Long-eared equine
5 Take in
6 D
7 Soft seat
8 There are two in a loaf
9 Part of an empire up to 1991: Abbr.
10 Crude group?
11 Send packing
12 Suffix with slug
15 Win in ___ (triumph easily)
17 "___ Amore"
18 "What ___ Believes" (Doobie Brothers hit)
22 Classic 1954 sci-fi film
23 Comet competitor
24 Telephone book, essentially
25 ___ fixe
26 Flash of light
27 Husband of Bathsheba
28 Slow times
29 City of Brittany
30 Violinist Zimbalist
34 Fury
35 Straw in the wind
37 Sunnis, e.g.
38 Hog, so to speak
40 Condoleezza Rice's department
41 New England catch
43 A de Mille
44 Set off
47 ___ cell research
48 Reduce to carbon
49 Word with fine or visual
50 "Dang!"
51 Make over
52 "___ example . . ."
53 Popular computer operating system
54 "Hold everything!"
55 Concerning
57 Ltr. addenda
58 "But I heard him exclaim, ___ . . ."

by Adam G. Perl

ACROSS

1 Put up, as a picture
5 ___ salts
10 Restaurant acronym
14 Fit for drafting
15 Mamma's mate
16 Shore bird
17 Headliner
18 Strand, as during a blizzard
19 Give a nudge, so to speak
20 "Take a chill pill"
23 CD predecessors
24 Conservative pundit Alan
25 Old copy machine, briefly
28 Pea's place
29 Exams for future attys.
33 Female in a flock
34 Whistle-blower on a court
35 Error
36 Out of it, as a boxer
40 Embedded
41 Witch
42 Stephen of "The Crying Game"
43 When some news airs
44 Like hearts and diamonds
45 Great time
47 Treated a lawn, perhaps
49 Winning tic-tac-toe row
50 Finally accept
57 Gave the boot
58 Pep up
59 Wax-coated cheese
60 Big rig
61 Singer Lopez
62 El ___ (Pacific Ocean phenomenon)
63 Ship's speed unit
64 Tennis champ Monica
65 Recipients of the cries seen at the starts of 20-, 36- and 50-Across and 7-Down

DOWN

1 "Bonanza" son
2 Opposed to
3 In order
4 Scramble, as a signal
5 Grand stories
6 Small indentation
7 "We were just talking about you"
8 Voiced a view
9 1975 Barry Manilow #1 hit
10 "Sure, why not"
11 Toss
12 Gymnast Korbut
13 Common movie house name ending
21 G.I.'s address
22 Excavation find
25 TV, radio, etc.
26 Words of refusal
27 Whimpers
28 Word before capita or annum
30 Integra maker
31 Adjusts, as a piano
32 Went after
34 Reel's partner
35 Ryan of "When Harry Met Sally"
37 Performed a routine perfectly
38 Mr. ___
39 Ate
44 Stop working at 65, say
45 Baseball's Jackson and others
46 Bargain-basement
48 Drops feathers
49 Old Dodges
50 Wine holder
51 Field team
52 Quick note
53 Philosopher Descartes
54 Peculiar: Prefix
55 Powdered drink mix
56 Med. care choices

by Jim Hyres

46

ACROSS

1 "Jaywalker" of late-night TV
5 C sharp equivalent
10 ___ Spumante
14 Worse than bad
15 Something coffee has
16 Golda of Israel
17 Leaves for cooking
18 About 39 inches
19 Scottish hillside
20 Coming attractions shot at a mobile home park?
23 It may be passed on the Hill
25 ___ Speedwagon
26 ___ work (road sign)
27 Full-length films shot at a day spa?
32 To any extent
33 Chafes
34 Lariat
35 Late civil rights pioneer Rosa
37 Gillette razor
41 "___ on Down the Road"
42 Throat malady
43 Film segments shot at an arsenal?
48 Ice cream sundae, e.g.
49 Eggs
50 Anka's "___ Beso"
51 Documentaries shot at a vacation paradise?
56 Did laps, say
57 Modern reading material
58 "Sorry about that!"
61 Fountain of jazz
62 Water ride
63 Expert
64 Iditarod entry
65 Like most manuscripts
66 On

DOWN

1 French article
2 "Deliver Us From ___," 2003 film
3 Nip before a tuck?
4 Table spread
5 Interest of a knight in shining armor
6 Without
7 Trent of the Senate
8 From the U.S.
9 Skater Lipinski
10 English novelist Eric
11 Unruffled
12 Jeweled coronets
13 "___ my case"
21 River to the Caspian
22 Don of morning radio
23 Many miles away
24 Roman statesman and writer
28 Spot of land in the Seine
29 Goofed
30 Diving bird
31 Superstation letters
35 Scorecard number
36 "___ was saying . . ."
37 U.S./Eur. divider
38 Auditions
39 Counts in the gym
40 Lhasa ___ (dog)
41 Words to Brutus
42 Surgery reminder
43 Embroidery yarn
44 Make fizzy
45 Rear-ended, e.g.
46 "Beat it!"
47 Brought forth
48 Kitchen measures: Abbr.
52 Skillful
53 Skillfully
54 Egg drop, e.g.
55 "Animal House" attire
59 For
60 "How's it hangin', bro?"

by Sarah Keller

ACROSS
1 Crop up
6 Service leader
11 Cricket club
14 Like some eclipses
15 Detective Pinkerton
16 "___ you sure?"
17 Amphitheater cover?
19 Contest of sorts
20 Sharp as a tack
21 Macadam ingredient
22 O'Neal of "Peyton Place"
23 Temperamental sort
25 Pitchfork features
27 Gore and Hirt
30 Coins found at a dig?
34 Takes off
36 Genetic letters
37 Engine unit
38 Swarm member
39 Spa offering
42 Lee of Marvel Comics
43 Packed away
45 Prospector's need
46 Julia's role in "Ocean's Twelve"
47 Prefight ceremony?
51 A.A.R.P. part: Abbr.
52 Overthrow, e.g.
53 Dirty look
55 Deimos orbits it
57 ___ Irvin, who designed the first cover for The New Yorker
59 On the hook
63 William Tell's canton
64 Calm at a wrestling match?
66 Pewter, in part
67 "___ World Turns"
68 Children's refrain
69 Put out
70 Questionnaire category
71 Played over

DOWN
1 Thomas ___ Edison
2 Wishes undone
3 J., F. or K.: Abbr.
4 Tijuana toast
5 Like the Kama Sutra
6 No-goodnik
7 Came to rest on a wire, e.g.
8 Sounds during wool-shearing
9 East Los Angeles, e.g.
10 Helpful contacts
11 Saturday night hire, often
12 Field
13 11-Down, frequently
18 They're dangerous when they're high
22 Stand up to
24 Ballerina Pavlova
26 Pro Bowl org.
27 Tattered Tom's creator
28 Maui neighbor
29 Little bit
31 Hose shade
32 Get on
33 Surrealist Max
35 Has the tiller
40 Picture holder
41 San ___, Tex.
44 Bergen's locale: Abbr.
48 Ranger's domain
49 Year-end decoration
50 Cow that hasn't had a cow
54 Flaxlike fiber
55 Kennel club rejectee
56 Star turn
58 Need an ice bag
60 Schooner filler
61 Luke Skywalker's sister
62 School on the Thames
64 Kung ___ chicken
65 Suffix with auction

by Randall J. Hartman

48

ACROSS

1 Tiff
5 Go out on the ocean
9 Bogged down
14 Letter before kappa
15 Longest river of Spain
16 "___ fired" (Trump catchphrase)
17 Classic holiday entertainment
20 In whatever way
21 Swing that rips the leather off the ball
22 "Waking ___ Devine" (1998 film)
23 Co. photo badges, e.g.
24 W.W. II female
26 Expectorate
28 Houston major-leaguer
30 Crouches
34 Amo, amas, ___ . . .
37 Morays
39 Dickens's ___ Heep
40 Shock
43 Three to one, e.g.
44 Nick and ___ Charles of "The Thin Man"
45 44-Across's dog
46 Lagoons' surroundings
48 Sleek fabric
50 "Too bad!"
52 Mos. and mos.
53 Clemson competes in it: Abbr.
56 Fit ___ fiddle
59 Horse feed
61 20 Questions category
63 "The Thin Man," for one
66 Bygone airline
67 Corner chesspiece
68 Sacked out
69 Sound made while sacked out
70 I's
71 Chess ending

DOWN

1 Biblical mount
2 Hit with a hammer
3 Lawyers: Abbr.
4 Dashboard dial, for short
5 Brine
6 Network of "Lost"
7 Nettles
8 Many movie houses
9 Magical aura
10 Letters of debt
11 Undo
12 Art Deco master
13 Monopoly card
18 Has the oars
19 Emulates Eminem
25 King of Thebes, in myth
27 Headdress that's wound
28 Head of the Huns
29 Actor Edward James ___
31 Is under the weather
32 Stretched tight
33 Queens stadium
34 Magician's opening
35 Castle protector
36 Choir voice
38 Leave the straight and narrow
41 Leader's cry, said with a wave
42 Where to hang derbies and fedoras
47 Volvo rival
49 "But there ___ joy in Mudville . . ."
51 Look steadily
53 Itsy-bitsy creature
54 West Pointer
55 Bonnie's partner in crime
56 Nile slitherers
57 Good, close look
58 Florence's river
60 Walk with difficulty
62 Mosque V.I.P.
64 Hearing aid
65 British john

by Jay Livingston

49

ACROSS

1 Poisonous plants
7 Letters for Letterman
10 "Right now!"
14 Discordant
15 Cry heard in a bullring
16 Small jet maker
17 Place to test aerodynamics
19 Isaac's eldest
20 Bakery gizmo
21 One of the Lennons
22 Broadway background
23 Hoopster Archibald
24 Kukla or Ollie, e.g.
28 Give it a go
30 Employ more employees
31 Glass marble
34 Clutch
37 Chinese author ___ Yutang
38 Placing (and a hint to the first words of 17-, 24-, 47- and 60-Across)
41 Stool pigeon
42 Out of style
43 Dull drills
44 2,000 pounds
46 Telepathic letters
47 Skinny Minnie
51 Funnyman Sandler
55 Offbeat
56 Some shortening
57 Brazilian soccer legend
58 Amorphous mass
60 Author's success
62 "La Bohème" heroine
63 Bit of sunshine
64 Practical
65 Direction wagon trains headed
66 Alias
67 Nebraska river

DOWN

1 Greeted, as the New Year
2 Central New York city
3 "Water Lilies" painter
4 Mario of the Indianapolis 500
5 Hipster
6 Like half-melted snow
7 Arthur ___ Doyle
8 It's not 100% this or that
9 French seasoning
10 Is in dreamland
11 Aviator in search of bugs
12 Battery size
13 Robert Morse Tony-winning role
18 PBS benefactor
22 Potluck get-togethers
25 Face, slangily
26 Some cyber-reading
27 Looks after
29 Give an answer
31 60's–70's dos
32 Goliath
33 Vestibules
34 Dogfaces
35 Hosp. staffers
36 Count of candles on a cake
39 "___ in there!"
40 Come to terms for less jail time, say
45 Gossip unit
46 Ultimately becomes
48 Dickens's "___ House"
49 Cushy course
50 Know-how
52 Blue-and-white earthenware
53 Alaskan native
54 Singer Haggard
58 Upscale auto initials
59 Practice tact, perhaps
60 Playtex offering
61 Immigrant's subj.

1	2	3	4	5	6	■	7	8	9	■	10	11	12	13
14						■	15			■	16			
17						18				■	19			
20				■	21				■	22			■	■
23				■	24				25				26	27
■	■	■	28	29		■	■	■	30					
31	32	33			■	34	35	36			■	37		
38					39						40			
41			■	42					■	43				
44			45			■	■	■	46			■	■	■
47						48	49	50		■	51	52	53	54
■	■	55			■	56				■	57			
58	59			■	60					61				
62				■	63			■	64					
65				■	66			■	67					

by Gail Grabowski and Nancy Salomon

50

ACROSS

1 See 24-Down
5 Easy ___
10 Mental keenness
14 Nebraska native
15 Unlikely to defect
16 "The Plague" city
17 Bandleader known for 55-Down
19 Seine feeder
20 Many Tyson finishes
21 Capek play
22 "Gullible's Travels" writer
24 URL ending
25 Cemetery, informally
26 Up
29 Judd of "Taxi"
30 Vestments, e.g.
31 Big jerk
32 1926 Channel swimmer
36 Suffix with psych-
37 Open, in a way
39 Start of many Hope/Crosby film titles
40 Philippine locale in W.W. II
42 ___ Gratia Artis
43 A bunch of
44 Absorbed, in a way
46 Krone spenders
47 Zigged and zagged
50 Door sign
51 Conestoga driver
52 Guff
53 Atlantic City mecca, with "the"
56 "Vidi," translated
57 Bandleader known for 47-Down
60 St. Petersburg's river
61 Kegger wear, maybe
62 "Mockingbird" singer Foxx
63 Colored like a certain hound
64 Blow hard
65 Daimler partner

DOWN

1 Varsity letter earner
2 Words of agreement
3 Part of R.S.V.P.
4 Poetic contraction
5 Vinyl collectible
6 Go parasailing
7 Cries of regret
8 Entruster of property
9 Under-the-sink items
10 Bandleader known for 25-Down
11 "Three Sisters" sister
12 Stun gun
13 Bergen dummy
18 Fox or turkey follower
23 Invoice abbr.
24 Bandleader known for 1-Across
25 See 10-Down
26 "A Girl, a Guy and ___" (1941 Ball movie)
27 "Later"
28 Old chap, say
29 Barbarous one
31 Lunch counter orders
33 Horse coloring
34 Pool path
35 Breyers rival
38 Verb with thou
41 Interminable time
45 Transplant
46 Johnny who played Willy Wonka
47 See 57-Across
48 Surgery tool
49 Tequila source
50 The "Divine" Bette
52 Cry in a mudslinging contest
53 Trident part
54 Call from the flock
55 See 17-Across
58 Actor Tognazzi
59 Thorax protector

by Ed Early

ACROSS
1 All excited
5 Unexpected sports outcome
10 Small salamander
14 Earring site
15 John who was once known as the Teflon Don
16 "That's clear"
17 Houston Astro, for one
19 Stare
20 Met production
21 Chart toppers
23 Dot-com's address
25 Ump's call
26 Actors not playing major parts
34 "Quiet, please!"
35 Disdain
36 Father Christmas
37 Sounds of relief
39 Keep after
41 ___ Piper
42 Bad way to run
44 Pigpens
46 Caribbean, e.g.
47 In the driver's seat
50 What to call an officer, maybe
51 Hither's partner
52 Where to get taxis
58 Comparison shopper's quest
62 Norway's capital
63 Not bad in result
65 Mix (up)
66 Laser printer powder
67 Diva Horne
68 Spinning toys
69 Winter falls
70 Historic periods

DOWN
1 Brand for Fido
2 Trail mix
3 Double-reed instrument
4 Get ready
5 "Yuck!"
6 Experts in vote-getting
7 Flower stalk
8 Jazz singer James
9 Attaches, as a rope
10 Bedtime drink
11 Actor Morales
12 Cried
13 Golf ball props
18 Field protectors
22 Holds close
24 ___ Ness monster
26 "Naughty, naughty!"
27 "Yeah"
28 Perch
29 It's a fact
30 Navel type
31 Biscotti flavoring
32 Girder material
33 "I did it!"
34 Swedish auto
38 Tailor's tool
40 Wet, as morning grass
43 Make a sweater
45 Rudely push
48 Pre-edited versions
49 Allow
52 Purchase price
53 Regarding
54 Radar image
55 It follows 11
56 First 007 film
57 One-dish meal
59 Suggestive look
60 School for a future ens.
61 J.F.K. postings
64 Mins. and mins.

by Marjorie Berg

52

ACROSS
1 Showman Ziegfeld
4 Shakespearean character who calls himself "a very foolish fond old man"
8 Traveler's baggage handler
14 Mary's boss on "The Mary Tyler Moore Show"
15 Writer Sarah ___ Jewett
16 Bogged down
17 Beer festival mo.
18 Musical staff symbol
19 Wanderers
20 Nickname for author Ernest
23 Prunes, once
24 France's Belle-___
25 Vegetarian's protein source
28 Abominable Snowman
29 Classic New York City eatery
32 Amtrak facility: Abbr.
34 Cartoonist Drake
35 Summer along the Seine
36 Paul McCartney in the Beatles
40 Not in stock yet
42 "So that's it!"
43 Milne's "The House at ___ Corner"
45 Anka's "___ Beso"
46 Fanny Brice radio character
49 Burst of wind
53 Greek peak
54 Card below quattro
55 Postal scale marking
56 This puzzle's theme
60 Photo assignments
62 "It's ___" ("I'm buying")
63 A couple of chips, maybe
64 Dawn goddess
65 ___ Martin (cognac brand)
66 Brenda of country music
67 Geological wonder
68 Madrid Mmes.
69 Wind up

DOWN
1 Disk type
2 Place
3 Yield
4 Scottish boating spots
5 ___ Stanley Gardner
6 What Procrit may treat
7 Uses another roll on
8 Symbol of troth
9 Sufficient, in poetry
10 Ex-senator Alfonse
11 Filled in a coloring book
12 I.R.S. exam: Abbr.
13 Sour cream container amts.
21 Not quite right
22 "Super!"
26 Big bash
27 ___-friendly
29 Lawyer created by 5-Down
30 Areas between shoulders?
31 Slugger Slaughter
33 Rewards for waiting
36 Popular clown at kids' parties
37 Teachers like to hear them
38 Long, drawn-out excuse
39 One end of a bridge
41 Scoundrel
44 "Egad!"
47 Louts
48 More acute
50 Not up to it
51 Sift
52 Tried out
55 Minds
57 To be, to Henri
58 Boris Godunov, e.g.
59 Madame Bovary
60 Droop
61 Ruby or emerald

by Sarah Keller

ACROSS
1 Spin doctor's concern
6 Mediterranean spewer
10 Sobriquet for Haydn
14 Gabbed away
15 Not fer
16 Drive away, as a thief?
17 With 21-Across, there's no . . .
19 Fall shade
20 Joanne of westerns
21 See 17-Across
23 Hard to miss
27 Sings in the Alps
28 Taters
29 It may be hard on a construction worker
32 Alley button
33 Dish served with a lemon wedge
34 Good source of potassium
36 There's no . . .
41 Brought up
42 "Little" boy of early comics
44 Bring a smile to
48 ___ Lingus
49 Take it off, take it all off
50 Shiny cotton fabric
52 "Told ya!"
54 With 59-Across, there's no . . .
57 "___ we there yet?"
58 School with King's Scholars
59 See 54-Across
64 Tabula ___
65 Asian princess
66 Company that took over Reynolds Metals in 2000
67 Lousy eggs?
68 Quartz type
69 Former Japanese capital

DOWN
1 Lyricist Gershwin
2 Raincoat, for short
3 Mandela's org.
4 "Sure, why not?!"
5 Accustoms
6 Bother, with "at"
7 Abbreviation said with a "Whew!"
8 Bogotá boy
9 Steamed
10 Memorial Day event
11 Takes advantage of, say
12 Mortar's partner
13 Swear (to)
18 Taker of vows
22 Service reading
23 Pressure cooker's sound
24 Each, slangily
25 Break in the action
26 Comedian's Muse
30 Licorice-scented herb
31 "Any ___?"
34 Arthur of "The Golden Girls"
35 ABC newsman Potter
37 Angler's basket
38 Sneakily
39 Trifling
40 Namer of a representative to OPEC, maybe
43 Unlock, to a poet
44 Rearward
45 Drink made with curaçao
46 Maximum
47 Interpreted to be
49 Run of luck
51 Funny-car fuel
53 Something that may be seen in a bank
55 Genghis ___
56 Start of a kid's counting rhyme
60 Fotos
61 Prefix with friendly
62 "___ so!"
63 The way of the Chinese

by Philip Thomson

54

ACROSS

1 Hunger twinge
5 Unpaid group of 7-Down
9 Sound heard hourly from Big Ben
14 Bassoon's little cousin
15 Nobelist Wiesel
16 Passenger
17 Bagpiper's wear
18 "___ Well That Ends Well"
19 Warn
20 Dutch cheese
21 Union: first stage
23 Label again, as a computer file
25 Put away for a rainy day
26 Money in South Africa
28 St. Francis' city
33 React like a threatened dog
36 Land on the Arabian Peninsula
39 Home for Adam and Eve
40 Put a cap on
41 One in a union with 37-Down
42 Lieu
43 "It's a sin to tell ___"
44 G.O.P. foes
45 Birthplace of the Renaissance
46 Interfere (with)
48 ___ of Sandwich
50 Voting no on
53 More profound
57 Union: second stage
62 100-meter race, e.g.
63 Precursor of the "Odyssey"
64 Reside (in)
65 Director Preminger
66 Washer cycle
67 Pizzeria fixture
68 City of waltzes, to natives
69 "Ciao!"
70 Overly bookish sort
71 Scent receiver

DOWN

1 Doc Holliday's game
2 Reside (in)
3 Actor Lloyd ___
4 Union: third stage
5 Overwhelm with sound
6 Jazzy Fitzgerald
7 See 5-Across
8 Physicist who pioneered alternating current electricity
9 Whooping birds
10 Site of Jack and Jill's spill
11 Prefix with -logue
12 Griffin who created "Jeopardy!"
13 Art Deco designer
22 "Terrible" czar
24 Brewer's ingredient
27 Damfool
29 Union: last stage
30 Genesis of an invention
31 Flippered mammal
32 ___ 500
33 Not shut quietly
34 Pharaoh's river
35 Surrounded by
37 One in a union with 41-Across
38 Cathedral recess
42 Beget
44 Post-Mao Chinese leader
47 NASA vehicle
49 The 3 or 5 in 3+5=8
51 Claw
52 "Uncle!"
54 Sunbather's spot
55 ___ Park, Colo.
56 Beaujolais's department
57 Lass
58 Kazan who directed "On the Waterfront"
59 Hue
60 Comfort
61 ". . . happily ___ after"

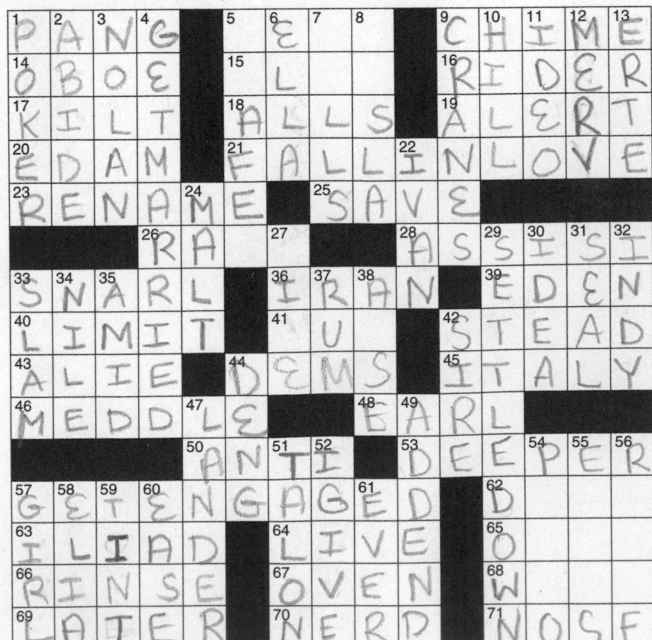

by Wesley Johnson

55

ACROSS

1 Stamp or coin collecting, e.g.
6 Artist Chagall
10 Men-only
14 "Fidelio," for one
15 Margarine
16 Frau's partner
17 Shouts of triumph
18 Rivers of comedy
19 "Green Gables" girl
20 Clueless reply
23 Hightail it
24 Statistics calculation
25 Camera type, briefly
27 Highway access
30 Squelch
34 Romances
36 Bump off
38 Skylit lobbies
39 Clueless reply
42 McQueen of "Bullitt"
43 52 cards
44 Brazilian soccer great
45 Con artists, slangily
47 Lose control on the highway
49 G-man or T-man
50 Pipe part
52 Continental currency
54 Clueless reply
60 Autobahn auto
61 Bound
62 Game for peewee batters
64 Brit's baby buggy
65 Brontë governess
66 New York Harbor's ___ Island
67 Rice wine
68 Monopoly acquisition
69 Edited out

DOWN

1 Supertrendy
2 Brightly colored fish
3 Pleasant place, metaphorically
4 Slugfest
5 Arafat of the P.L.O.
6 Voodoo spell
7 Outfielder Moises
8 Royal domain
9 Purchased apartments
10 Beatles command, baby, in "Twist and Shout"
11 Dollywood's state: Abbr.
12 Florence's river
13 Got bigger
21 Intoxicating
22 G.I.'s neckwear
25 Nothing-but-net sound
26 Numbers game
28 State of mind
29 Evergreens
31 Slugfest
32 Fine cotton fabric
33 Lightened (up)
35 Uses a shortcut
37 Head/shoulders connector
40 "Doggone!"
41 Powder lover
46 Ready for mailing, as an envelope
48 Checked for prints
51 "That's hogwash!"
53 Moscow money
54 Mushroom toppers
55 Ambience
56 Bismarck's home: Abbr.
57 Cabby's client
58 Newspaper's ___ page
59 Writer Wiesel
63 Psychedelic of the 60's

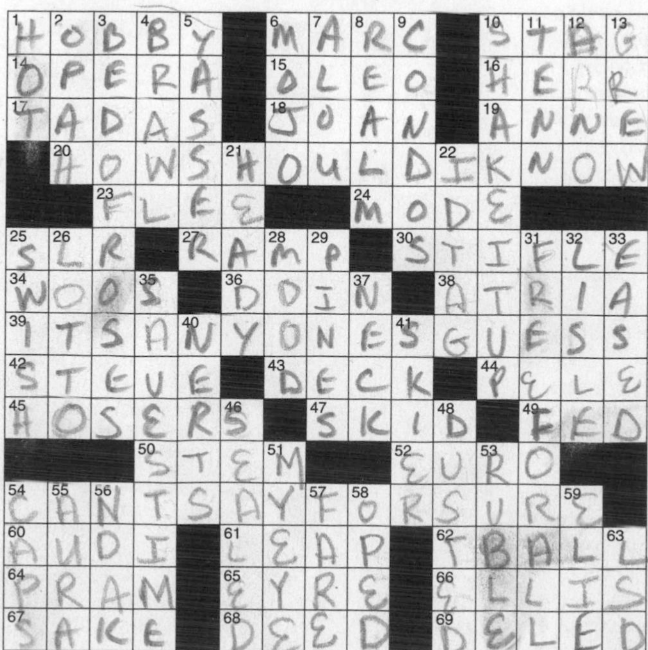

by Nancy Salomon

56

ACROSS

1 One-liner, e.g.
5 Fighting
9 Fabrics for uniforms
14 Golden rule preposition
15 Canon creator
16 "That smarts!"
17 Depict a card game?
19 Hawke of film
20 "___ Fly Now" ("Rocky" theme)
21 Genesis locale
23 Believer's suffix
24 Sign-off
25 "CSI" airer
27 1976 Sally Field role
30 Depict an improv routine?
34 Rah-rah sort
36 Illusory works
37 James Brown's genre
38 Foul moods
41 Like centenarians
42 Scintillas
44 Holstein, e.g.
46 Depict part of the periodic table?
49 "Cool!"
50 "Concentration" pronoun
51 Lose zip
54 Down
56 One more time
58 Shaping tool
60 Confesses
63 Depict suds?
65 Site of Joan of Arc's demise
66 Hideous sort
67 Show one's teeth?
68 Chip maker
69 "Forget about it"
70 Christian Science founder

DOWN

1 Dog show V.I.P.
2 Ken Lay's company
3 Put up with
4 Crier's place
5 Blood typing system
6 Pauses
7 Knocked off, in a way
8 Beat, as wheat
9 Salon item
10 Raise a stink?
11 Way back when
12 Diagonal
13 Posted, say
18 Baseball card buys
22 Where B'way is
26 Track action
28 "You stink!"
29 Airbag activator
30 Comfort giver
31 It may be organized
32 Keene sleuth
33 Ongoing accounting fig.
34 Knuckle-dragger
35 Utter
37 Pose
39 Sci-fi subject, or a 1970's dance
40 Knocked off, in a way
43 Lunar plain
45 Kowtowed
47 Zeta follower
48 "White Fang" author
51 Knight's need
52 On top
53 Far from sterile
54 Delhi wrap
55 Doorbell-ringing company
57 "It follows that . . ."
59 French religious title
61 Minute
62 The Coneheads' show, for short
64 Ticket add-on

by Levi Denham

57

ACROSS

1 Take hold of
6 Anatomical pouches
10 "___ Excited" (Pointer Sisters hit)
14 Severity
15 Melville novel
16 Alcove
17 First president born outside the original 13 colonies
19 Easy tennis shots
20 Retirees, often
22 A Chaplin
23 Norma ___, Sally Field Oscar-winning role
24 Mentally sharp
26 Revolution time?
28 Ewe's mate
31 Often ___
32 Long time
35 Airhead
37 April 15 org.
38 B team
42 Driveway covering
43 Leslie Caron title role
44 Fleming who created 007
45 Shaquille of the N.B.A.
47 Kind of camera: Abbr.
49 Catch sight of
53 Kind of acid
55 Yellowstone Park animal
58 "Mazel ___!"
59 They're neither nobility nor clergy
63 Horse's hue
64 Bad way to be held by a judge
65 007 foe
66 Scheme
67 Suffered defeat, slangily
68 "I'd hate to break up ___"
69 MS. enclosure
70 Zellweger of "Bridget Jones's Diary"

DOWN

1 Lawnlike
2 Hearty steak
3 List for a meeting
4 Songs for one
5 Before, with "to"
6 World Cup sport
7 Mine, in France
8 Stallion, once
9 Actress Braga
10 Coast features
11 Frank Zappa's daughter
12 Sympathy-arousing excuse
13 Approves
18 Gun lovers' org.
21 One of the Gabors
25 S.A.T. company
27 Stimpy's pal on TV
29 Aleve competitor
30 "Mamma ___!"
33 Like some old-fashioned lamps
34 "___ won't!"
36 Prefix with angle
38 Mop wielders
39 Foam material
40 "Treasure Island" author's inits.
41 Suffix with labyrinth
42 Bridge weight unit
46 Retort to "Am too!"
48 Decorated anew
50 Place for pollen
51 Entree with a crust
52 Actress Mimieux
54 Poker pieces
56 Actor Cariou
57 Relatively cool sun
60 "To Live and Die ___"
61 Certain TV's
62 French head
63 Nutritionist's fig.

by Kevan Chosel

58

ACROSS
1 Antisub weapon, slangily
7 Boarded up
11 Atty.'s title
14 Composer Debussy
15 Hawaiian fish, on menus
16 Thanksgiving, e.g.: Abbr.
17 1984 campaign slogan
19 ___ polloi
20 Descartes's "therefore"
21 Graceful woman
22 Folk singer Joan
23 Actresses Ireland and St. John
24 1980's White House nickname
25 The "E" in Alfred E. Smith
29 Classic drugstore name
32 Animated Disney heroine of 1998
33 Main artery
36 Sign before Virgo
37 Song from "Anything Goes"
40 Ordinal suffix
41 Dens
42 Ryan of "The Beverly Hillbillies"
43 Rotary phone user
45 Pump figures
47 Family girl
48 Bring back to court
50 Samsung or RCA product
52 In a way, slangily
53 Brewer's kiln
57 Boise's state: Abbr.
58 1975 #1 disco hit
60 It can hold its liquor
61 John Lennon's "Dear ___"
62 Mideast market
63 Hurricane center
64 Frankenstein's helper
65 Come into view

DOWN
1 Farm division
2 Talk like a drunk
3 Nail to the wall
4 Stephen King canine
5 Sidewalk stand quaff
6 Storied monster, in tabloids
7 Suspect
8 Angels' strings
9 "No way!"
10 Oscar statuette, mostly
11 Green Mountain Boys leader
12 Clog or pump
13 20 questions, say
18 Course outlines
22 Go rounds in a ring
23 Lions' "kingdoms"
24 "The Apprentice" TV genre
25 War correspondent, in modern lingo
26 Prefix with task
27 Hawaii's nickname
28 Slangy refusal
29 MapQuest offering: Abbr.
30 Sierra ___
31 Home Depot competitor
34 Bruins great Bobby
35 Italian dish cooked in broth
38 Berne's river
39 Woman's support system?
44 Roman 54
46 Buster of Flash Gordon serials
48 Columnist Mike
49 Unwanted computer message
50 Center of activity
51 June 6, 1944
52 Trudge
53 Élève's 11
54 Miles away
55 Smeltery refuse
56 Radial for a Jaguar, e.g.
58 Memo-opening letters
59 Descartes's "sum"

by Adam Cohen

ACROSS
1 1980's Chrysler product
5 Totally lost
10 No-goodniks
14 Coin tossed in the 15-Across fountain, nowadays
15 "Three coins . . ." fountain
16 Genesis victim
17 Unwelcome visitor
19 "Friends" spin-off
20 "My Cousin Vinny" star
21 Wavy design
22 Duplicates, for short
25 Totally crush
28 They may be pulled off
30 Blue-ribbon
31 Likewise
32 Good thing to be in
34 Some four-year degs.
37 Fellow in a 1944 Johnny Mercer song hinted at by 17-, 25-, 47- and 57-Across
41 Worker's check
42 Photo finish
43 ___ Domini
44 Jumbo, for one
45 Miscellaneous task
47 Tenacity
52 Treasury div.
53 Dodge 1-Across
54 V formation members
56 Rolling rock?
57 Like a bad apple
62 Highlight?
63 Fragrant resin
64 Maven
65 Fish caught in pots
66 Hem in
67 Fall locale

DOWN
1 Bud holder, maybe
2 Mangy mutt
3 ___ Ben Canaan, Leon Uris hero
4 Nail-biter's opposite
5 Bikini events
6 Tiny amount
7 Photo tone
8 67-Across figure
9 It's inspired
10 Wheedle
11 Bubbling
12 Combine name
13 More artful
18 Not play
21 Painter of haystacks
22 Rocky, twice
23 Salsa queen Cruz
24 Weenie
26 Weasel word
27 Reader's goal
29 Slurrer, perhaps
32 See 57-Down
33 Report letters?
34 1970's cinematic canine
35 ___ Wences
36 Hoity-toity sorts
38 Eastern V.I.P.'s
39 Bring down
40 Roll of dough
44 Drags through the mud
45 Moving on, say
46 1950's sitcom name
47 Like some starts
48 Ticked off
49 Ken-L Ration competitor
50 Cruel sorts
51 "C'mon, my turn!"
55 Rim . . . or trim
57 With 32-Down, places to browse
58 Cry of approval
59 Broadway nightmare
60 Before of yore
61 Wimple wearer

by Seth A. Abel

60

ACROSS
1 Inclement
6 "Let me know if ___ help"
10 "Damn Yankees" siren
14 Mrs. Kramden of "The Honeymooners"
15 Grp. that outlasted the Warsaw Pact
16 Sacred bird of the pharaohs
17 Rock bottom
18 Gator's cousin
19 Captain for 40 days and nights
20 Wisconsin pro footballer
23 Craze
24 Wedge-shaped inlet
25 Reconstruction outsider
32 Length of 14⅔ football fields
35 George Bush's home state
36 Fashion magazine
37 Airport flight info: Abbr.
38 Wine cask
39 Can.'s southern neighbor
40 Trucker's rig
42 Freeway sign with an arrow
44 Consider
45 Golden Gloves participant
48 Big inits. in long distance
49 Opposite of absorb
52 Center of Mt. St. Helens
58 Crèche figures
59 Brilliant star
60 Play much too broadly on stage
61 Stewpot
62 26- or 55-Down
63 Joe of the Yankees
64 Hammer's end
65 "Auld Lang ___"
66 Underhanded sort

DOWN
1 Send to the gallows
2 Morning waker-upper
3 "___ cock-horse to Banbury Cross"
4 Biology or chemistry
5 Rupture
6 Old Peruvian
7 Actor Grant
8 Perched on
9 Diet food catchphrase
10 Connection
11 Penetrating wind
12 Fibber
13 Close-grained wood
21 One of TV's Simpsons
22 Undercover org.
26 Russia's ___ the Great
27 Bedroom community
28 Activity for which "it takes two"
29 Stickum
30 ". . . or ___!" (threat)
31 Paper purchase
32 Small plateau
33 Any thing
34 Holy man of Tibet
41 From Tuscany, e.g.
42 Sci-fi creatures
43 Company bigwig
44 "Yeah, sure!"
46 List ender
47 Wading birds
50 Workplace for the person named at the end of 20-, 25-, 45- or 52-Across
51 Half of octa-
52 Place between hills
53 Look at long . . . and with longing
54 Prying
55 ___ the Terrible
56 Org. helping people in need
57 Smell
58 Implement in a bucket

by Gary Steinmehl

ACROSS

1 Angelic music maker
5 Think ahead
9 San Diego baseballer
14 Parkay product
15 Capital of Italia
16 Instruments used in orchestra tuning
17 Pronto
20 Sack material
21 ". . . or ___ just me?"
22 Dallas-to-Duluth dir.
23 Place to hear snorts
24 Family M.D.'s
26 Adds or deletes text
28 Pronto
32 E. Lansing school
34 "Platoon" setting
35 Hoodwink
36 French roast
37 Snatches
40 Lahr who played the Cowardly Lion
41 Smooth-barked tree
43 Shoot the breeze
44 Promising words
45 Pronto
49 Skin layer
50 Head lines?: Abbr.
51 "20/20" network
54 Prince ___ Khan
56 Loony
58 Sweetums
60 Pronto
63 Area, weatherwise
64 Rebuke from Caesar
65 Latest thing
66 Calculus symbol
67 Haul in
68 Desire personified

DOWN

1 Roy ___, lead role in "The Natural"
2 Native Alaskan
3 Cook, as beans
4 Certain hotel amenity
5 Getting ready
6 Moviedom's Myrna
7 Mine, on the Marne
8 Sartre novel
9 Bonneville maker
10 Blood-typing system
11 Smaller now, in corporate-speak
12 Check, with "in"
13 Italian Renaissance art patron
18 Prego competitor
19 Rug rats
25 Lasting impression
27 Small-time
28 Lunch dish from the oven
29 S. S. Kresge, today
30 Whodunit hero Wolfe
31 Round Table title: Abbr.
32 Big name in faucets
33 Reliable source of income for a band
36 Suicide squeeze stat.
38 Innocent
39 Puts the pedal to the metal
42 Celestial Seasonings beverage
46 Part of a Latin I conjugation
47 Kind of
48 Pulitzer-winning writer James
51 Loud, as a crowd
52 "That's it!"
53 Hands over
54 Travels like a skyrocket
55 "___ Marlene," song of 1944
57 Web spot
59 Fair-sized garden
61 "Well, let me see . . ."
62 Tkt. office locale

by Nancy Salomon

62

ACROSS

1 Busch Gardens locale
6 Enervates
10 Tête-à-tête
14 Modern source of pass-along jokes
15 Legal claim
16 Too smooth
17 For the ___
18 "Things are great for me"
20 Long march
21 Hotfooted it
22 Little laugh
23 #1 hit for the Crystals
25 Eerie ability
26 Pay, with "up"
27 Belief system
29 C.I.A. forerunner
32 Odds and ends
35 Serengeti sighting
36 Vitriol
37 "Quit cryin' "
40 Mailed
41 Whole lot
42 Does toe loops, e.g.
43 Army Corps of Engrs. supply
44 Source of an androgyne's confusion
45 Window ledge
46 Alley ___
48 Kipling's comment about "The Liner"
53 "Peter and the Wolf" bird's name
55 Suffragist Carrie Chapman ___
56 Award for Samuel Beckett
57 Track cry after "and"
59 "Absolutely Fabulous" mom
60 "Aha!"
61 Old Harper's Bazaar illustrator
62 Abacus wielder
63 Curtain holders
64 ___-majesté
65 Netizens

DOWN

1 Tithing fraction
2 Subject for an Italian aria
3 Prides of lions?
4 Criticize analytically
5 Happy hour order
6 Pass
7 Evangelist ___ Semple McPherson
8 Pitching, in a way
9 ___-Cat
10 Two-scoopers, e.g.
11 Acme
12 Lip balm ingredient
13 Little kid
19 Particular
21 Able to feel
24 One may be skipped
28 Get by (on)
30 Sour fruit
31 Finishes, with "up"
32 DOS part: Abbr.
33 "Fargo" director
34 Deteriorate
35 Martini ingredient
36 Undoubtedly
38 Game summary
39 Tulsa's locale: Abbr.
44 Butt heads
45 Fixed charge
47 "That's for sure"
49 Weapon handles
50 "___ With Me" (popular hymn)
51 Car on a train
52 A long time
53 Hurly-burly
54 "I get it now"
58 Fish lacking a pelvic fin
59 ___ de Cologne

by Manny Nosowsky

ACROSS

1 ___ Bearcat (classic car)
6 Muslim leader
10 Cover the driveway
14 Gdansk natives
15 "I Just Wanna Stop" singer ___ Vannelli
16 Manipulator
17 How often rent is usually paid
19 Perlman of "Cheers"
20 1950's prez
21 It's nothing at all
22 Herb with the Tijuana Brass
24 Oldtime crooner Julius
26 What a settlement avoids
28 Indian music
30 Difficult situations
34 "My Friend ___" (old radio/TV series)
37 Frozen waffle brand
39 Lovable ogre of film
40 Bellyache
41 What each of the longest words in 17A, 65A, 10D and 25D famously lacks
43 Online auction site
44 Mexican friend
46 MasterCard alternative, informally
47 Inquires (about)
48 Kodaks, e.g.
50 Crowd reaction
52 Jokes
54 " " " " "
58 Rocket propulsion
61 Pudding fruit
63 Blood-typing letters
64 Second-largest of the Hawaiian islands
65 Lone Ranger's cry
68 Writer Waugh
69 ___ synthesizer
70 Din
71 Small winning margin
72 Diarist Frank
73 Xenon and neon

DOWN

1 Go bad
2 Toy truck maker
3 Stomach malady
4 Golf ball raiser
5 A Gabor sister
6 Stravinsky or Sikorsky
7 North Dakota city
8 Picnic intruder
9 Angora fabric
10 Military hero's award
11 ___ Stadium (Queens landmark)
12 Suddenly change course
13 Part of Q.E.D.
18 Scanty
23 Young fellows
25 Breakfast beverage
27 Boardinghouse guest
29 Shocked
31 Wall St. figures
32 Plumbing problem
33 "The ___ the limit!"
34 Apple computer
35 Italia's capital
36 Seriously injure
38 Sock hop locale
42 Large-scale emigration
45 Underground deposits
49 Respiratory problem
51 Pointing
53 Observe furtively
55 Smiley of PBS
56 Fatter than fat
57 Tender areas
58 Fed. agent in finances
59 Saint's glow
60 Regrets
62 Seating section
66 Charged particle
67 Mauna ___ volcano

by Allan E. Parrish

64

ACROSS

1 Urban pollution
5 Booster, to a rocket
10 Winter home of the Chicago Cubs
14 Volcanic flow
15 Hang in the air
16 "We deliver for you" sloganeer: Abbr.
17 Ruthless personnel director
18 The Hunter
19 Genesis twin
20 Seasoned dancer?
23 Frequently
24 Austrian peaks, locally
28 Ancient writing material
31 Spacecraft to Jupiter
33 Missed by ___ (was way off)
34 Mantra sounds
35 Cockpit datum: Abbr.
36 Seasoned singer?
41 Missing button on an iPod: Abbr.
42 Monday night game org.
43 Extra, as a bedroom
44 The Washington Monument, e.g.
47 Emily Dickinson's home, in Massachusetts
49 Police weapon
50 Bridge authority Charles
51 Seasoned baseball player?
57 Portend
60 ___-ground missile
61 Anise-flavored liqueur
62 Sierra Club co-founder
63 ___-O-Matic (baseball game company)
64 Sitting on
65 Victories
66 Approval power
67 "Yo, ___!"

DOWN

1 Waste material
2 Passé skirt style
3 Breadmaking place
4 Quaint building decoration
5 Vowel sound in "puzzle"
6 Spanish constructions
7 Par ___ (how to send mail to France)
8 Atlas maker's subj.
9 White-tailed eagle
10 Nutritious breakfast cereal
11 Double curve
12 Resort
13 Tempe sch.
21 ___ Zimbalist Jr.
22 "Too-ra-loo-ra-loo-___"
25 Two-dimensional
26 Conger catchers
27 Possible answer to "Are we there now?"
28 Polly, who wants a cracker
29 Protozoan
30 Sign after Aquarius
31 Maker of Yukon SUV's: Abbr.
32 Communication for the deaf: Abbr.
34 Olive ___
37 Opposite of a ques.
38 Washington's ___ Stadium
39 Milo of "Barbarella"
40 Route that invites speeding
45 Pariahs
46 Rage
47 Main arteries
48 Peter Lorre role in eight movies
50 President Ford, informally
52 Free ticket
53 Round bread
54 Ballet attire
55 Popular shirt label
56 "Uh-uh!"
57 Autobahn auto
58 Yes, in Québec
59 Clamor

by Roy Leban

ACROSS
1 Tear open
6 Made like
10 Take on
14 Composer Camille Saint-___
15 Farming community, e.g.
17 Camel
19 Legal matter
20 "Uh-oh"
21 Still in the game
22 Averse to
25 Made square
26 Embryonic sac
27 It may be rounded up in a roundup
29 Iona athletes
30 Postage purchase
31 End of another actor's line, maybe
34 Camel
38 W. Hemisphere group
39 A deadly sin
40 Tilter's tool
41 In accord (with)
43 Lewd
44 Stiff
47 It may be drawn
48 Quaking tree
49 NBC's "My Name Is ___"
51 Figs.
53 Camel
57 Elementary particles
58 Go leisurely
59 Wool caps
60 Night fliers
61 Jenny Lind, e.g.

DOWN
1 SALT party
2 Goya masterwork, with "The"
3 They make sense
4 Abbr. on a bank statement
5 Tire letters
6 It's inert
7 Heart, essentially
8 Big times
9 "Dapper" one
10 Semi, e.g.
11 Monte of Cooperstown
12 One of Chaucer's pilgrims
13 Like some seals
16 Split
18 Eight bells
23 Bit of trickery
24 ___ Parker
25 They're caught in pots
26 Soil: Prefix
27 Work out
28 Sizable
30 Hockey's ___ Smythe Trophy
31 Asian cuisine
32 Plain
33 Barbara who played a TV genie
35 It's inert
36 "Gil ___"
37 Go ballistic
41 Pros
42 Lowish voice
43 Uncontrolled
44 "It ___ me!"
45 "The Verdict" actor, 1982
46 It may be found in a den
47 Reporter's badge
49 Italy's Mt. ___
50 On ___ streak (winning)
52 Eye woe
54 Not be entirely truthful
55 Type widths
56 Scatter

by James R. Leeds

66

ACROSS

1 Borrow without intending to repay
6 College administrator
10 Eyebrow shape
14 Oak's source
15 Former attorney general Janet
16 Hawaiian feast
17 Terrific
18 Cupid's Greek counterpart
19 Ancient Peruvian
20 Part of a famous 1897 editorial
23 Author Fleming
24 Delete
25 Christmas drink
27 Christmas trimming
30 First 007 film
31 Tree's anchor
32 Ballet movement in which the knees are bent
35 Went out, as the tide
39 "Lord, is ___?"
40 Editorial, part 2
42 Swiss river to the Rhine
43 Analyze grammatically
45 Prefix with nautical
46 Thomas ___ Edison
47 Quickly, in memos
49 Spice in Christmas cookies
51 Christmas songs
54 River around the Île de la Cité
56 Attorneys' org.
57 Editorial, part 3
62 Prima donna
64 "Things aren't looking good"
65 City NNE of Paris
66 Detail
67 Greedy person's cry
68 Prudential competitor
69 Philosopher known as "the Stoic"
70 Observer
71 Vision of sugar-plums dancing in one's head, e.g.

DOWN

1 Sly
2 Farming unit
3 Executes
4 Most serious
5 Complete
6 Lees
7 Like a ghost's howling
8 Ever and ___
9 More meddlesome
10 He KO'd Foreman in '74
11 Altercation
12 Tree that's the source of chocolate
13 Second-longest river of China
21 Kramden of "The Honeymooners"
22 "___ of God," 1985 film
26 Sailor, slangily
27 Misstep
28 Greek "I"
29 Film ___
30 Rudolph and team
33 Spring
34 Anger
36 Unguent
37 Roof overhang
38 Pull behind
40 Edison rival
41 Ancient Greek colony
44 ___ Paulo, Brazil
46 Artist's workplace
48 Take for granted
50 In one's birthday suit
51 Port of Spain
52 Have ___ to eat
53 Poe bird
54 Keep others awake at night, maybe
55 Upper atmosphere
58 Cry to a matey
59 Germany's Konrad Adenauer, Der ___
60 Bone near the radius
61 Stitching line
63 ___, amas, amat . . .

by Richard Hughes

ACROSS
1 Command to Rover
5 Feudal estate
9 Veronica of "Hill Street Blues"
14 Jai ___
15 Not taken in by
16 Stubborn as ___
17 British man-of-war
19 Bulgaria's capital
20 On a higher plane
21 Above everything else
23 Formerly, formerly
25 Nuns' garb
26 Knuckleheads
29 Neighbor of Francia
32 Landed
33 Yellow fruit
34 Nice winter coat
37 Man o' War
40 Dam-building org.
41 Comparatively close
42 "What's in a ___?": Juliet
43 It's gender
44 Kafka's "In the ___ Colony"
45 The Supreme Court, e.g.
48 Lowly worker
50 Place for things to get sorted out
53 Home in bed, ill
57 In other words
58 Portuguese man-of-war
60 Copier company
61 Natural balm
62 Three-point shot, in hoops slang
63 "Danse Macabre" composer Saint-___
64 Card catalog abbr.
65 Towel embroidery

DOWN
1 "Stop! You're killing me!"
2 Trees in an O'Neill title
3 "___ of Eden"
4 Opera script
5 They're not fair
6 Place to overnight
7 Jazz singer James
8 A. J., the racer
9 Rosh ___
10 One-celled creature
11 Civilian attire
12 "Middlemarch" author
13 Bounds' partner
18 Pair in a dinghy
22 "Casey at the Bat" writer Ernest Lawrence ___
24 Treat roughly
26 A bit cuckoo
27 Sainted Norwegian king
28 Capital near the ruins of the ancient city Pachacamac
30 Bowler's pickup
31 Indiana hoopsters
33 False start?
34 Friend of Kukla and Ollie
35 Alma mater of D.D.E.
36 Virginia dance
38 Brings to light
39 20%
43 A Rockefeller
44 Supplicate
45 Mideast princes
46 Gymnast Comaneci
47 Family girl
49 Sitcom that debuted in 1994
51 Town near Santa Barbara
52 Blanc and Brooks
54 Kind of need
55 Word with fee or ID
56 ___ Ed.
59 High ball?

by Nancy and Holden Baker

68

ACROSS

1 Corday's victim
6 Billiard shot
11 Convenience store sign
14 Classic game company
15 Like World Cup crowds
16 Charles X, e.g.
17 59-Across and others
19 Dispenser of 47-Across
20 Irritate
21 Where to spend kips
22 Mid fourth-century year
24 Results of ties: Abbr.
25 ___-Hawley Tariff Act of 1930
26 Cheer
27 Shelley's "___ Skylark"
28 Old Chevy
31 Professional grp.
34 Comment made while fanning oneself
37 Cyclades island
38 Classic Dickens title (from whose 10 letters this puzzle was constructed)
41 ___ polloi
42 Itsy bits
43 Must
44 Casual walk
46 Show
47 See 19-Across
48 Commandment word
51 ___ Poly
54 Wreck
56 Sail supporter
57 Colombian city
58 Coach Parseghian
59 Ebenezer Scrooge player in a 1951 movie version of 38-Across
62 ___ chi ch'uan
63 Conductor Georg
64 Portuguese colony until 1999
65 Entirely
66 Kind of energy
67 Pile up

DOWN

1 Introduction to economics?
2 On ___ (carousing)
3 "Groundhog Day" director
4 Seed covering
5 Start of a winning combination
6 Major export of Ivory Coast
7 Movie droid, familiarly
8 Perch
9 Stick in the water
10 Tiny Tim's mother in 38-Across
11 Places for theorizers?
12 Shed item
13 Rodolfo's love in "La Bohème"
18 ___ mater
23 Suffix with mini or Web
25 Working poor, e.g., in 38-Across
27 Rocky hill
28 1980's–90's TV nickname
29 Cheer (for)
30 Kon-Tiki Museum site
31 Cries of delight
32 59-Across, e.g.
33 It's usually tucked in
34 "Am ___ believe . . . ?"
35 "Dee-lish!"
36 Joke responses
39 Cards, on the scoreboard
40 Berne's river
45 Commercial suffix with Rock
46 Utah ski resort
48 Trivial
49 "___ mañana"
50 Moving
51 Conspirator against Caesar
52 Popular spy show
53 Line at an airport
54 "Bye now"
55 Spoken
57 Jampack
60 John
61 "Well, ___ monkey's uncle!"

by David J. Kahn

ACROSS

1 "A guy walks into a ___ . . ."
4 State Farm competitor
9 French artist Edgar
14 From ___ Z
15 Start of a weightlifting maneuver
16 ___ Gay (W.W. II plane)
17 Wail
18 1994 John Travolta film
20 Unordinary
22 Mended, as socks
23 Litter's littlest
24 Boob tube, in Britain
26 Damon of "Good Will Hunting"
28 O_3
30 Suffix with Oktober
34 Swiss peak
35 Mouse catchers
36 Defense grp., 1954–77
37 Dentists' focus
39 Tire pressure measure: Abbr.
40 Varnish ingredient
41 The "E" of EGBDF
42 Sponsorship
44 "We Know Drama" cable channel
45 Actress Ward
46 British guns
47 McDonald's arches, e.g.
48 Place
50 Bridge guru Sharif
52 Friend of Betty and Veronica, in the comics
55 Wine server
58 "Queen of Hearts" vocalist, 1981
61 Neither's partner
62 Place to exchange rings
63 Boutiques
64 "Little" car in a 1964 top 10 hit
65 Bridle straps
66 Competitive, as a personality
67 Mind-reading ability, for short

DOWN

1 Low voice
2 Sitting on
3 British leader from whom the "bobbies" got their name
4 Former defense secretary Les
5 Line that extends for 24,902 miles
6 1960's–80's rock group Jethro ___
7 Short snooze
8 Fed. law enforcement org.
9 Toy race car adornment
10 Price to participate
11 Enter
12 Skin cream additive
13 Hourglass fill
19 Doing nothing
21 Last word from a director
24 Tournament favorite
25 Coast Guard rank
26 Pub buddies
27 Tylenol rival
29 Mexican revolutionary Emiliano
31 City neighboring Newark, N.J.
32 Bee injury
33 Kemo Sabe's sidekick
35 "___ kingdom come . . ."
36 Some S.A.T. takers
38 Refuse holder
43 Heavy hydrogen, e.g.
46 Witnessed
47 Perry Mason's profession
49 Stadium levels
51 High-I.Q. set
52 Open slightly
53 Govern
54 Commercial prefix with bank
55 "Halt!"
56 Goes bad
57 Plunge
59 Guinness Book suffix
60 "How come?"

by Allan E. Parrish

70

ACROSS

1 Biblical gift-givers
5 Tattle (on)
9 Knight's "suit"
14 "Ain't that the truth!"
15 Where to get off
16 Lorna of literature
17 Flier of coffee for long distances?
19 "___ luck!"
20 Big 60's dos
21 Flustered state
22 Fleet leader
25 1981 Julie Andrews movie
26 Martians, e.g., in brief
27 Author A. Conan ___
28 Bleep out
30 Surgery ctrs.
31 Steps out of France
34 Not completely closed
37 Loco
39 Sound heard in 17- and 58-Across and 11- and 24-Down
40 Grenade part
41 Kind of engr.
42 Hoofing it
44 "This ___ test"
45 Long arms?
47 Went like a shooting star
49 Ottoman governor
51 TV spots
52 Fearful feeling
54 Private gag
56 Corners
57 Alla ___ (music notation)
58 High school grads?
62 The one with 0 in 7-0
63 Not much
64 Craving
65 Bookkeeping task
66 1936 Jean Harlow title role
67 Pizazz

DOWN

1 Capt.'s superior
2 Te ___ cigars
3 "How about that?!"
4 Behind bars
5 Cousin of quadri-
6 Praise to the rafters
7 Empty promises
8 Word unit: Abbr.
9 Wings it
10 Tooth part
11 Milk?
12 Early stages
13 Brings up
18 Violinist Zimbalist
21 "Stick around!"
22 Clay for bricks
23 Miami stop on the P.G.A. Tour
24 Witticism from Sherlock Holmes?
25 Take care of
28 Sleeve ends
29 Clumsy sort
32 Tristan's love
33 Canonical hour
35 Intelligence or good looks, e.g.
36 "Set?"
38 Chem. or bio.
43 They may be graduated
46 Smoke and mirrors
48 Off-color
49 Perennial best seller, with "the"
50 Noted bankruptcy of 2001
52 Ball's partner
53 Lacking lucre
55 "Back to you"
56 Dancer's dress
58 Essen assents
59 Electronic address
60 Turkish title
61 Cub Scout group

by Lee Glickstein and Nancy Salomon

ACROSS
1 Symbol of blackness
5 Stone of many Libras
9 Radio-active one?
13 Excessive indulgence
14 Monte ___
15 Some learning
16 Take it on the lam
18 ___ Barak, former Israeli P.M.
19 Sport fisherman's catch
20 Coffee-flavored liqueur
22 Dash
24 Toon's place
27 It's occasionally 5
28 Part of a stereo player
32 Dollar rival
34 Deviate
37 Hideous one
38 Bolt
41 Diuretic's target
42 Place to brood
43 Crate part
44 Make even deeper
45 Grp. formed in Bogotá
47 Cheer syllable
48 Scoot
53 Lamp filler
56 Yule scene
60 Lionel layout, maybe
61 Skedaddle
63 Building toy brand
64 John of the Broncos
65 Susan B. Anthony's goal
66 Give ___ for one's money
67 Punta del ___, Uruguay
68 River of Flanders

DOWN
1 Go for
2 Sea predator
3 Thickening agent
4 A serous fluid
5 Stroke's need
6 First: Prefix
7 "Cavalleria Rusticana" baritone
8 Lite
9 Some Halloween costumes
10 1922 Physics Nobelist
11 Place for pins
12 Hester Prynne's stigma
14 Chump change, abroad
17 Inside dope
21 Musical Miller
23 Aerosol gas
24 Handle the food for a party
25 Duck
26 Went for
29 Seasonal airs
30 China's Zhou ___
31 Doesn't play
33 Pause indicator
35 Suffix with benz-
36 Surface anew
39 Lisbon's river
40 Like taro or sago
46 "No sweat"
49 [Titter]
50 Dye-yielding plants
51 Cereal box fig.
52 Having chutzpah
53 Stimulating nut
54 "Did you ___?"
55 Prego competitor
57 ___ Bay, Ore.
58 Kind of mail
59 Linda of Broadway
62 ___ Bo (exercise system)

by Ernest Lampert

72

ACROSS

1 Actor Baldwin
5 Go a mile a minute, say
10 Canaanite god
14 Length between mini and maxi
15 Uptight person
16 Peter ___, classic cartoonist for The New Yorker
17 One's equal
18 Dances at Jewish weddings
19 Alliance since '49
20 1852 book
23 Old Italian money
24 Long, long time
25 1944 play
31 Trap
32 Low-cal
33 Miner's find
35 Egyptian fertility goddess
36 Takes a turn on "Wheel of Fortune"
38 Unadulterated
39 "Queen of denial" for Queen of the Nile
40 Ollie's partner in old comedy
41 Wild
42 1992 movie
46 Actor Chaney
47 Classical paintings
48 1970's TV show with a literal hint to 20-, 25- and 42-Across
55 Feeling that makes you say "Ow!"
56 Biblical spy
57 When repeated, a court cry
59 For men only
60 The Little Mermaid
61 The "N" of N.B.
62 "Dear God!"
63 Pee Wee who was nicknamed the Little Colonel
64 Quick cut

DOWN

1 Unit of current, informally
2 In ___ of (instead of)
3 Home for Adam and Eve
4 Vultures, at times
5 Globe
6 For the time being
7 Currency that replaced 23-Across
8 Dutch cheese
9 Puddings and pies, e.g.
10 Snack for a monkey
11 Saudi, e.g.
12 Not for
13 Crazy as a ___
21 Fertilizer ingredient
22 Arrive
25 "To recap . . ."
26 Wet, weatherwise
27 Thin pancakes
28 "Ich bin ___ Berliner"
29 Grieve
30 Lineup
31 Taste, as wine
34 Sushi fish
36 Vehicle that does crazy tricks
37 ___ de deux
38 Funds for retirees
40 Shortly
41 What soap may leave
43 Tight, as clothes
44 Bank's ad come-on
45 Practical, as a plan
48 Lhasa ___ (dog)
49 Homebuilder's strip
50 Actor Neeson
51 Long-eared leaper
52 Nobelist Wiesel
53 City on the Rhône
54 Abominable Snowman
58 Microwave

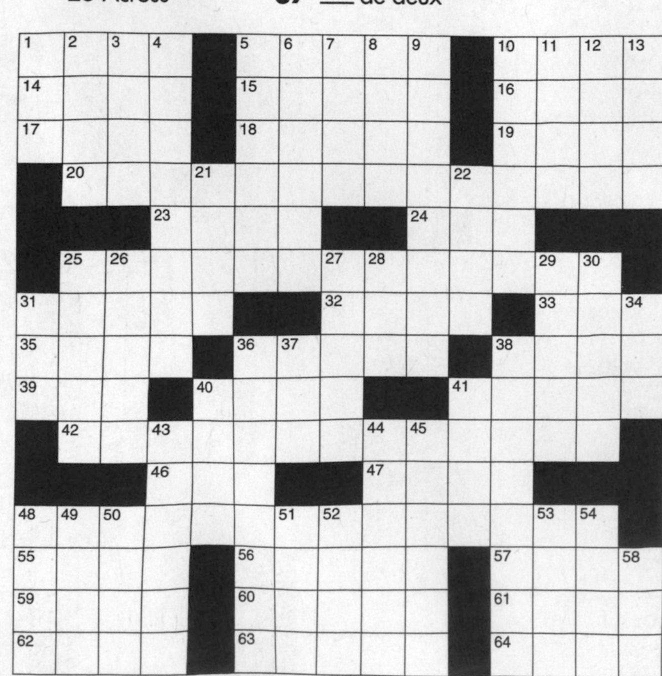

by Linda Schechet Tucker

73

ACROSS

1 Serf's oppressor
5 Pirate Lafitte
9 Joe ___ (average guy)
14 Numbered work
15 Competent
16 Butter maker
17 Drink for Vanna?
19 Funny O'Donnell
20 Augusta National members
21 Rob ___ (drink with Scotch)
22 Caught some Z's
24 Novelist Lurie
26 Regulation for Natalie?
29 Cold place?
30 Barbarian of the comics
31 Potato feature
32 Wilts
33 Critique harshly
34 Fools around (with)
36 Dessert for Edith?
39 Roundup rope
42 Form 1040 org.
43 Shade providers
47 Prez on a fiver
48 Sharp-tasting
50 Enough
51 Family for Pearl?
53 Appreciative diner
54 Diarist Nin
55 Kipling hero
56 Sales worker, for short
57 Give the O.K.
59 Sound quality for George?
62 River's end, sometimes
63 Soothing gel ingredient
64 Place to broil
65 Scaredy-cat
66 Pen points
67 Plain writing

DOWN

1 Catholic rite that lacks singing
2 Tragic figure in "Hamlet"
3 Spoiling
4 P.M. brightener
5 Chief Argonaut
6 Auction site
7 Entirely
8 "Schindler's List" star
9 Airport anti-terrorism worker
10 Cuts (up)
11 Disco dances
12 Certain hosp. test
13 Solitary
18 Cupid, to the Greeks
23 Andes climbers
25 Kind of bar
26 Hand over, as for sale
27 Senate vote
28 General Clark, to friends
30 Knave
33 Three-term New York governor
35 Step (on)
37 Erodes
38 Attempt
39 Family dog, for short
40 Baghdad's ___ Ghraib prison
41 Consumer safety measures
44 Give the go-ahead
45 Sniffler's supply
46 Garden of Eden inhabitant
49 Sentra maker
50 Prepares to shoot
52 Comb stoppers
53 Moon-related phenomena
55 Radio dial
57 Madison Ave. output
58 Oahu memento
60 ___ Baba
61 Young'un

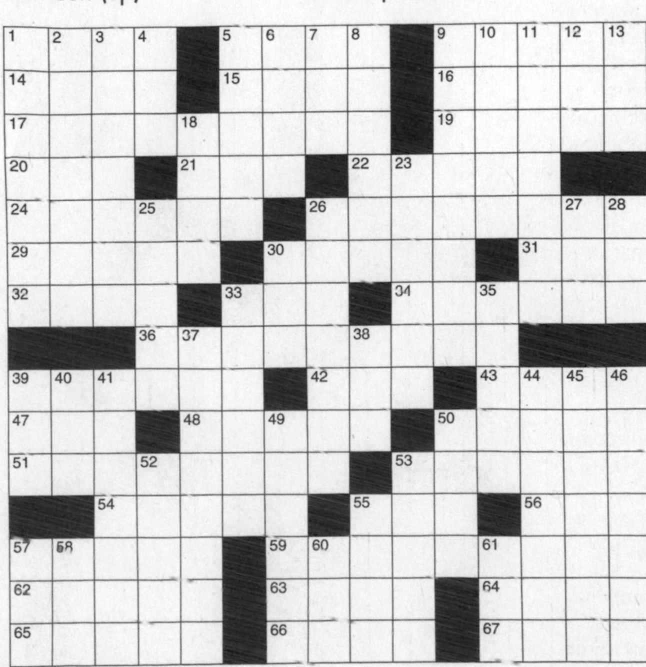

by Lynn Lempel

74

ACROSS

1 Freighter or whaler
5 Read cursorily
9 Chick's cries
14 Window section
15 Prefix with sphere
16 Uncredited actor
17 Rocketeer
19 Writer Joyce Carol ___
20 Cheerleader's cheer
21 Novelty dance spawned by a 1962 #1 hit
23 CD player
25 Freudian ___
26 Reach by foot
29 Certain fir
33 "I love," in France
35 "___ perpetua" (Idaho's motto)
37 Raison d'___
38 Holder of funerary ashes
39 What the ends of 21- and 57-Across and 3- and 30-Down all name
42 Leading pitcher
43 Close by, in poetry
45 Words of enlightenment
46 Goose egg
48 Less difficult
50 Have high hopes
52 Nickname for Dallas
54 Fiats
57 Party bowlful
62 "___ la la!"
63 Lenin's middle name
64 Big business-related
66 Small recess
67 "What is to be done?!"
68 Kind of tea
69 "___ With Love" (1967 hit)
70 Wild hog
71 Units of resistance

DOWN

1 Poles on a 1-Across
2 Attacks
3 Waiting just out of sight
4 The "p" of m.p.h.
5 Dope
6 New Jersey's ___ University
7 Don of talk radio
8 Hands, in slang
9 Central Illinois city
10 Case in point
11 Blues singer ___ James
12 F.D.R. or J.F.K.
13 Window frame
18 Dish often served with home fries
22 Rudely poke
24 St. Louis gridder
27 "___ of the D'Urbervilles"
28 Actor Milo
30 Old West transport
31 St. Louis landmark
32 Get together
33 Beaver's mom on "Leave It to Beaver"
34 Opera highlight
36 "Little piggies"
40 Sign of late summer
41 Declared
44 Small patio grill
47 Mentalist Geller
49 A choice word
51 Jalapeño, to name one
53 1983 Mr. T flick
55 Pole carving
56 Outbuildings
57 Blood donation, maybe
58 Mishmash
59 Tiny spasms
60 Popular cream-filled cake
61 "My Friend ___" of old radio/TV
65 Brazilian getaway

by Allan E. Parrish

ACROSS

1 Basics
5 Raft wood
10 Goes (for)
14 Christine ___ (29-Down's love)
15 Leave stranded by a winter storm
16 One who says "I say, old chap"
17 See 11-Down
18 It crashes in 29-Down/ 60-Across
20 Seethes
22 Reverse of WNW
23 Site of Margaret Mead studies
24 With 40- and 51-Across, composer of 29-Down/ 60-Across, as well as 63-Across
26 Position
27 End a suit
30 Oboist's need
31 ___ Stadium, home of the U.S. Open
32 Theater areas
36 Old spy org.
39 Addict
40 See 24-Across
41 Aware of
42 Slice (off)
43 Toy gun ammo
44 Condo, e.g.
45 When repeated, words of agreement
47 Communion tables
49 Famed fireman Red
51 See 24-Across
54 Buddhist temple sights
55 "___ had it!"
56 Persistently worry
60 See 29-Down
63 Longest-running show in Broadway history until 1/9/06
64 Cheer (for)
65 Painter Matisse
66 Real name of 29-Down
67 West Point team
68 Hot, blue spectral type
69 Salon supplies

DOWN

1 Attaches
2 Can of worms?
3 Spelunking site
4 Brine
5 Pen name
6 One who's sore
7 Place for a renter's signature
8 Tendon
9 Now ___ then
10 Flattened at the poles
11 Carlotta, in 29-Down/ 60-Across
12 Fasten, as a ribbon
13 Costly strings
19 Twisty curves
21 NBC fixture since '75
25 Casino worker
27 Fellow named Bellow
28 Petrol provider
29 With 60-Across, longest-running show in Broadway history as of 1/9/06
30 Levi's jeans brand
33 Indisposed
34 Peruvian money
35 Soap ingredient
37 Cookbook direction
38 Tipplers
41 Went faster than
43 Examine grammatically
46 You might get a ticket for doing this
48 Novelist Deighton
49 Old marketplace
50 Help with
51 Wetnaps, e.g.
52 Happening
53 Quotable Yogi
57 Indiana city near Chicago
58 Play to ___
59 Sounds of disapproval
61 "So there you are!"
62 Put on TV

by David J. Kahn

The Complete Line of Light and Easy New York Times Crossword Puzzles

Easy to Solve...Hard to Resist!

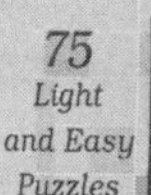

Edited by Will Shortz

Available at your local bookstore or online at
nytimes.com/nytstore.

St. Martin's Griffin

1

2

MINTS FICA KILN
ASEAT ADAM WEAR
IMHIP ROSA AIWA
NEILARMSTRONG
BUYS AAR HST
RESALE ANNA THE
ERIC BRETT YON
WALKEDONTHEMOON
ASH LISAS ANTI
REO BETZ CARESS
DRU OSO BAEZ
EDWINALDRINJR
SATO RILE APIAN
OCTO AVON TANIA
BEER EYED ENOLS

3

JIBE SHARI EKED
USES TOXIN DELE
SWEPTASIDE APSE
TET AGES PESTER
SALMON TUNA
OREO AVID RETRO
BOTANY ERICA
UPS PEPTALK TAR
PATTI ORDEAL
CLARA ROSA EACH
MITT RATTLE
RIPLEY MANX TAD
ONTO PTAMEETING
BRAG EAGER URGE
SEXY SPINS BESS

4

BLOGS TAFFY CIA
ROMEO ALICE AMS
ONETWOPUNCH RPI
WINS TIM UMPED
MOON TADPOLE
IMPALES INIGO
MEARA TKO LAB
PARTNERSINCRIME
SNL VEE RANIN
OWNED SNAGGED
FORWARD TEMP
LOGIC AMO ARIA
IMA HUFFANDPUFF
RPM OGLER DELFT
THE SHOWY TREYS

5

6

B	R	A	T	S	■	B	A	S	K	S	■	A	S	I
A	D	O	R	E	■	O	R	O	N	O	■	N	H	L
M	A	K	E	A	N	O	F	F	E	R	■	D	E	L
■	■	■	S	N	A	G	■	T	E	E	T	H	E	S
P	A	W	S	■	P	I	E	S	■	■	O	O	N	A
O	R	E	■	M	E	E	T	H	A	L	F	W	A	Y
M	E	D	E	A	■	■	S	O	N	O	F	■	■	■
P	A	S	T	D	U	E	■	E	G	G	E	D	O	N
■	■	■	C	A	N	N	Y	■	■	E	E	R	I	E
C	O	M	E	T	O	T	E	R	M	S	■	N	N	W
A	B	I	T	■	■	R	A	R	E	■	R	O	K	S
C	O	N	C	I	S	E	■	A	S	T	A	■	■	■
T	I	C	■	S	E	A	L	T	H	E	D	E	A	L
U	S	E	■	A	R	T	I	E	■	M	A	G	N	A
S	T	D	■	K	E	Y	E	D	■	P	R	O	N	G

7

S	T	R	A	P	■	D	A	N	E	■	K	A	L	E
T	H	E	M	E	■	O	R	A	L	■	A	X	I	S
A	R	I	E	L	■	G	E	R	I	■	H	O	S	T
R	U	N	N	I	N	G	A	C	C	O	U	N	T	■
■	■	■	■	C	I	I	■	■	I	A	N	■	■	■
P	R	I	V	A	T	E	E	N	T	R	A	N	C	E
L	I	N	E	N	■	■	M	O	E	S	■	A	O	L
A	C	N	E	■	H	E	A	R	D	■	L	O	C	I
I	C	E	■	S	I	M	I	■	■	S	A	M	O	A
D	I	R	T	Y	P	O	L	I	T	I	C	I	A	N
■	■	■	R	N	S	■	■	N	I	A	■	■	■	■
■	P	R	A	C	T	I	C	A	L	M	A	G	I	C
L	O	O	N	■	E	D	E	N	■	E	L	I	Z	A
B	L	O	C	■	R	O	B	E	■	S	E	N	O	R
J	O	K	E	■	S	L	U	R	■	E	G	A	D	S

8

S	L	U	G	S	■	B	L	T	■	A	B	E	T	S
G	E	N	O	A	■	L	O	O	■	L	E	N	I	N
T	W	O	B	Y	F	O	U	R	■	L	A	D	L	E
■	■	■	A	E	O	N	S	■	R	E	M	O	T	E
H	U	N	D	R	E	D	Y	E	A	R	S	W	A	R
I	S	O	■	S	S	E	■	M	I	G	■	S	T	S
F	E	T	E	■	■	■	V	I	S	I	T	■	■	■
I	D	E	M	A	N	D	A	R	E	C	O	U	N	T
■	■	■	S	P	O	I	L	■	■	■	O	R	E	O
A	T	A	■	P	R	E	■	S	S	S	■	G	A	P
T	H	R	E	E	M	U	S	K	E	T	E	E	R	S
L	E	M	A	N	S	■	C	I	R	R	I	■	■	■
A	W	O	R	D	■	T	H	E	B	I	G	T	E	N
S	H	U	N	T	■	H	E	R	■	P	H	O	T	O
T	O	R	S	O	■	Y	D	S	■	S	T	E	A	D

9

H	A	T	S	■	V	I	L	A	■	R	O	P	E	S
I	L	I	E	■	A	X	E	L	■	A	L	L	A	H
F	A	L	A	■	S	N	I	T	■	G	E	E	S	E
I	S	T	H	A	T	A	F	A	C	T	■	A	Y	E
■	■	■	A	B	L	Y	■	R	O	A	R	S	A	T
A	N	Y	W	A	Y	■	B	R	O	G	U	E	■	■
H	O	O	K	S	■	S	E	A	R	■	E	G	G	S
A	P	U	■	H	I	T	L	I	S	T	■	O	A	T
B	E	D	S	■	S	I	L	L	■	B	O	O	Z	E
■	■	O	R	A	L	L	Y	■	S	O	N	N	E	T
M	I	N	I	M	A	L	■	X	E	N	A	■	■	■
E	D	T	■	I	M	L	I	S	T	E	N	I	N	G
N	O	S	E	D	■	I	G	O	T	■	D	O	E	R
S	L	A	Y	S	■	F	O	U	L	■	O	N	E	A
A	S	Y	E	T	■	E	R	T	E	■	N	A	R	Y

10

J	I	V	E	■	S	P	L	I	C	E	■	B	I	C
I	N	I	T	■	A	L	A	N	O	N	■	E	S	O
B	R	E	A	D	B	A	S	K	E	T	■	L	T	R
S	E	S	S	I	O	N	S	■	R	E	T	T	O	N
■	■	■	M	T	S	■	S	C	R	U	B	■	■	■
S	U	D	S	E	S	■	Q	U	I	E	T	U	D	E
C	L	O	T	S	■	R	A	Z	O	R	■	C	A	L
A	N	G	E	■	F	I	T	I	N	■	S	K	I	M
L	A	B	■	S	E	T	A	E	■	B	A	L	S	A
P	R	I	S	O	N	E	R	■	B	O	L	E	Y	N
■	■	■	S	L	U	G	S	■	S	A	X	■	■	■
R	E	C	A	P	S	■	T	A	K	E	C	A	R	E
E	A	U	■	C	H	O	W	D	E	R	H	E	A	D
M	R	I	■	A	U	P	A	I	R	■	U	R	G	E
O	P	T	■	N	I	P	S	E	Y	■	M	O	E	N

11

L	A	D	E		G	E	N	T	S		R	O	T	C
E	N	I	D		A	G	O	R	A		E	M	I	L
A	D	A	M		T	A	R	O	S		A	N	N	A
D	E	N	O	T	E	D	M	U	S	I	C	I	A	N
	S	A	N	E				P	E	R	T			
			D	E	P	O	S	E	D	M	O	D	E	L
W	A	C		D	O	D	O			A	R	O	S	E
A	L	O	T		L	E	N	D	S		S	C	A	N
N	O	I	R	E			I	C	E	D		S	I	T
D	E	F	I	L	E	D	C	L	E	R	K			
			B	A	S	E				E	E	L	S	
D	E	B	U	N	K	E	D	P	R	I	V	A	T	E
A	T	I	T		I	D	A	H	O		I	B	E	X
Z	O	N	E		M	E	D	I	T		N	E	V	E
E	N	D	S		O	R	A	L	S		S	L	E	D

12

E	M	I	R			M	O	D	E	M		A	B	C
M	I	S	E	R		A	B	O	V	E		T	O	O
U	N	E	M	O	T	I	O	N	A	L		L	O	P
S	T	E	A	M	Y		E	S	S		M	A	Z	E
			P	E	S	O	S		I	R	I	S	E	S
A	S	H		R	O	D		A	V	E	R			
M	N	E	M	O	N	I	C	D	E	V	I	C	E	S
M	A	M	A			O	O	H			A	R	I	A
O	P	P	O	R	T	U	N	E	M	O	M	E	N	T
			R	Y	E	S		R	A	N		W	E	E
S	P	H	I	N	X		K	E	Y	E	D			
H	O	E	S		T	A	U		A	D	O	R	E	D
A	K	A		F	I	N	D	I	N	G	N	E	M	O
R	E	D		E	L	T	O	N		E	U	B	I	E
P	R	Y		W	E	I	S	S			T	A	T	S

13

T	U	B	A		B	E	D	S		P	A	T	S	Y
U	R	A	L		O	M	A	N		A	D	I	E	U
G	I	S	T		T	A	R	A		S	L	E	E	K
	S	H	O	O	T	I	N	G	S	T	A	R	R	
				I	L	L			A	R	I			
T	R	I	P	L	E		M	A	N	Y		S	I	S
E	E	R	I	E		P	A	C	T		E	T	N	A
N	E	A	N	D	E	R	T	H	A	L	M	A	N	N
E	S	T	E		N	O	T	E		A	I	R	E	D
T	E	E		A	D	D	S		A	L	T	E	R	S
			O	R	E			A	V	A				
	W	O	R	L	D	W	I	D	E	W	E	B	B	
G	E	N	I	E		O	D	O	R		V	A	I	L
A	N	T	O	N		R	E	P	S		E	R	T	E
S	T	O	N	E		K	A	T	E		N	E	E	D

14

A	T	T	N		A	M	A	Z	E		G	R	I	P
T	H	E	O		R	E	M	I	T		R	E	A	R
T	E	N	T		E	R	A	T	O		O	L	D	E
A	W	N		W	A	I	T	I	N	G	G	A	M	E
C	H	I	C	E	S	T				A	S	T	I	N
H	O	S	E	D		S	L	A	P	S		I	T	E
			L	G	E		A	L	L		A	V	I	D
	T	E	L	E	V	I	S	I	O	N	S	E	T	
Y	O	Y	O		I	R	E		T	E	A			
E	R	E		C	L	A	R	K		A	M	A	S	S
S	T	E	R	N				E	A	T	I	N	T	O
M	I	X	A	N	D	M	A	T	C	H		Y	A	W
A	L	A	N		E	A	R	T	H		L	O	C	H
A	L	M	A		E	M	I	L	E		A	N	K	A
M	A	S	T		D	A	Z	E	D		B	E	S	T

15

Z	A	P	P	A		P	A	S	H	A		J	E	T
E	T	H	A	N		I	S	L	E	T		O	R	E
B	E	A	T	T	H	E	H	E	A	T		S	I	N
R	U	S	H	E	E			W	R	I	T	H	E	D
A	P	E	S		R	C	A		T	R	I			
				S	E	A	L	T	H	E	D	E	A	L
P	L	U	M	E		S	I	R	S		B	A	R	E
R	E	R	U	N		T	B	A		S	I	R	E	N
O	V	A	L		S	L	A	G		A	T	L	A	S
F	I	L	L	T	H	E	B	I	L	L				
			A	H	A		A	C	E		M	A	Y	S
A	F	G	H	A	N	S			C	L	I	Q	U	E
F	L	U		T	A	K	E	T	H	E	C	A	K	E
R	E	F		I	N	A	W	E		A	R	B	O	R
O	A	F		S	A	T	E	D		R	O	A	N	S

16

F	L	E	C	K	■	T	E	E	S	■	A	H	A	B
S	A	T	I	E	■	A	X	L	E	■	L	O	L	A
T	R	A	V	E	L	V	I	S	A	■	B	R	E	T
O	V	I	■	P	O	E	T	■	L	A	U	N	C	H
P	A	L	O	M	A	R	■	P	E	R	M	S	■	■
■	■	■	T	U	N	N	E	L	V	I	S	I	O	N
■	S	L	I	M	■	■	L	I	E	D	■	N	B	A
B	O	A	S	■	H	O	V	E	L	■	H	O	O	P
A	H	S	■	B	A	L	I	■	■	G	E	N	E	■
H	O	T	E	L	V	I	S	I	T	O	R	■	■	■
■	■	P	R	E	E	N	■	N	O	T	A	B	I	T
S	A	L	A	D	A	■	S	L	O	E	■	A	R	E
E	R	A	S	■	S	T	E	E	L	V	I	S	O	R
R	A	C	E	■	A	R	A	T	■	E	D	E	N	S
F	L	E	D	■	Y	A	M	S	■	N	O	R	S	E

17

G	A	F	F	■	R	A	B	B	I	■	B	O	M	B
E	B	R	O	■	E	V	I	A	N	■	O	L	I	O
A	L	E	X	T	H	E	O	R	D	I	N	A	R	Y
R	Y	E	■	H	A	N	S	E	■	M	I	N	E	D
■	■	■	Z	A	S	U	■	■	A	M	T	■	■	■
P	E	T	E	T	H	E	M	E	D	I	O	C	R	E
R	A	I	N	S	■	■	A	P	E	X	■	L	O	X
O	T	T	O	■	L	A	Y	I	N	■	B	O	D	E
O	E	R	■	S	A	G	A	■	■	A	L	T	E	R
F	R	E	D	T	H	E	N	O	T	S	O	H	O	T
■	■	■	O	U	R	■	■	P	O	S	T	■	■	■
S	T	E	R	N	■	P	O	I	S	E	■	A	P	B
K	A	T	E	T	H	E	P	A	S	S	A	B	L	E
I	M	A	M	■	O	R	A	T	E	■	D	O	I	N
D	E	L	I	■	P	U	L	E	D	■	S	U	E	Z

18

C	O	R	P	S	■	P	O	L	L	■	S	T	O	P
O	F	A	R	C	■	A	P	I	A	■	H	A	R	I
M	A	Y	O	R	■	G	E	N	T	L	E	M	A	N
■	■	■	P	A	T	O	N	T	H	E	B	A	C	K
S	T	O	O	P	E	D	■	■	■	V	A	L	L	I
P	E	T	S	E	M	A	T	A	R	Y	■	E	E	E
A	D	I	E	U	■	■	U	P	N	■	■	■	■	■
S	S	S	■	P	I	T	B	O	S	S	■	M	I	T
■	■	■	■	■	T	O	E	■	■	U	S	E	N	O
E	M	T	■	P	O	T	S	T	A	R	T	E	R	S
S	O	A	M	I	■	■	■	S	P	R	I	T	E	S
P	U	T	O	N	E	O	V	E	R	O	N	■	■	■
I	N	T	R	A	N	S	I	T	■	U	G	L	I	S
E	D	E	N	■	O	H	O	S	■	N	E	E	D	Y
S	S	R	S	■	W	A	L	E	■	D	R	I	E	R

19

R	A	B	B	I	■	T	O	T	O	■	P	H	A	T
E	L	L	E	N	■	A	P	E	X	■	A	E	R	O
E	L	A	N	D	■	K	E	N	O	■	R	A	C	Y
S	A	R	D	I	N	E	C	A	N	A	R	D	■	■
E	Y	E	■	R	E	F	■	N	I	N	■	B	A	A
■	■	■	T	A	X	I	S	T	A	N	D	A	R	D
G	A	I	A	■	T	V	A	■	N	A	R	N	I	A
L	I	N	T	■	■	E	N	D	■	■	O	D	E	R
A	M	O	E	B	A	■	T	O	T	■	I	S	L	E
S	A	C	R	E	D	C	O	W	A	R	D	■	■	■
S	T	U	■	E	V	A	■	N	B	A	■	T	W	A
■	■	L	A	T	E	S	T	B	U	Z	Z	A	R	D
S	P	A	M	■	R	H	E	E	■	O	H	G	O	D
P	E	T	E	■	S	E	R	A	■	R	O	U	T	E
A	P	E	S	■	E	D	I	T	■	S	U	P	E	R

20

B	I	C	S	■	E	A	S	Y	■	F	R	O	Z	E
A	N	A	T	■	A	R	E	A	■	L	E	X	U	S
S	E	V	E	R	T	I	E	S	■	A	T	I	L	T
I	P	A	N	A	■	■	T	I	E	R	■	D	U	E
S	T	L	■	R	E	M	O	R	S	E	L	E	S	S
■	■	C	R	E	T	E	■	■	Q	U	O	■	■	■
E	S	A	I	■	T	A	I	L	■	P	A	W	E	D
L	A	D	Y	T	E	N	N	I	S	S	T	A	R	S
S	P	E	A	R	■	Y	E	A	H	■	H	I	R	T
■	■	■	D	A	M	■	■	R	O	S	E	S	■	■
N	O	T	H	I	N	G	I	S	O	N	■	T	N	T
E	M	U	■	P	O	U	R	■	■	A	B	B	I	E
W	A	R	E	S	■	S	K	I	N	G	R	A	F	T
S	H	O	V	E	■	T	E	L	E	■	A	N	T	E
Y	A	W	E	D	■	O	D	E	D	■	E	D	Y	S

21

S	H	A	Q		S	H	I	P	S		G	A	B	S
P	E	R	U		P	E	R	O	T		O	P	A	L
A	N	T	E		A	R	M	O	R		M	E	N	U
			B	A	R	B	A	R	A	B	O	X	E	R
E	T	H	E	L				E	W	E	R			
J	O	E	C	O	C	K	E	R		D	R	A	M	S
E	R	A		T	A	I	L		D	E	A	D	O	N
C	E	R	F		S	N	I	P	E		H	A	T	E
T	U	T	O	R	S		Z	A	S	U		G	E	E
S	P	Y	R	I		M	A	R	K	S	P	I	T	Z
			S	N	C	C				A	R	O	S	E
I	T	S	A	D	O	G	S	L	I	F	E			
T	A	C	K		D	R	A	I	N		P	R	A	M
C	L	U	E		A	A	R	O	N		P	O	L	O
H	E	M	S		S	W	A	N	S		Y	E	L	P

22

C	H	E	V	Y		S	H	A	Q		S	P	O	T
A	E	R	I	E		T	O	F	U		T	E	A	R
P	R	I	V	A	T	E	P	R	O	P	E	R	T	Y
O	R	C	A		O	R	S	O		A	P	S	E	S
			L	Y	O	N			A	R	D	E	N	T
H	I	D	D	E	N	A	G	E	N	D	A			
A	V	A	I	L			A	R	K		D	E	J	A
W	A	R		P	A	N	G	R	A	M		C	U	B
K	N	E	E		R	O	N			E	P	O	D	E
			S	E	C	R	E	T	B	A	L	L	O	T
C	A	R	O	M	S			A	L	D	A			
A	L	I	B	I		Z	U	L	U		T	Y	C	O
C	O	V	E	R	T	O	P	E	R	A	T	I	O	N
T	O	E	S		A	N	O	N		S	E	P	A	L
I	F	S	O		G	E	N	T		P	R	E	X	Y

23

A	N	G	E	S		S	C	R	O	D		C	O	T
D	A	R	I	A		P	I	A	N	O		R	F	K
A	R	E	N	A		O	T	T	E	R		U	F	O
P	R	E	S	B	Y	T	E	R	I	A	N	S		
T	O	N			O	T	R	A			E	A	V	E
S	W	E	E	T	L	Y		C	R	A	W	D	A	D
			L	O	A		S	E	A	T		E	T	S
	B	R	I	T	N	E	Y	S	P	E	A	R	S	
P	E	A		A	D	D	S		S	A	C			
J	A	I	A	L	A	I		A	T	M	C	A	R	D
S	U	N	G			F	E	T	A			M	A	I
		B	E	S	T	I	N	P	R	A	Y	E	R	S
C	E	O		L	O	C	A	L		D	O	L	E	S
P	A	W		A	R	E	C	A		A	R	I	S	E
A	U	S		T	E	S	T	Y		M	E	A	T	S

24

R	A	J			S	P	E	W		S	A	G	A	S
S	P	U	R		P	O	R	E		T	R	A	M	P
V	A	L	E		A	O	N	E		R	A	Z	O	R
P	R	E	F	E	R	R	E	D	S	A	L	A	R	Y
S	T	P	E	T	E			Y	O	W				
			R	A	K	E	S		S	H	I	P	T	O
A	T	M	E		E	L	L	A		A	N	E	A	R
T	H	A	N	K	Y	O	U	L	E	T	T	E	R	S
T	R	I	C	E		N	E	I	N		E	S	S	O
N	O	N	E	E	D		S	A	T	Y	R			
				P	I	P			R	E	V	S	U	P
J	O	B	A	P	P	L	I	C	A	T	I	O	N	S
A	R	O	M	A		U	N	P	C		E	L	B	A
M	A	N	I	C		S	T	A	T		W	A	I	T
B	L	A	D	E		H	O	S	E			R	D	S

25

A	R	C	O		D	E	L	F	T		N	E	M	O
S	A	H	L		E	M	I	L	E		O	X	E	N
S	H	E	L		S	O	L	A	R		N	I	N	E
	R	E	A	L	I	T	Y	B	I	T	E	S		
N	A	T		I	R	E				E	T	T	A	S
C	H	A	R	L	E	S	T	O	N	C	H	E	W	S
O	S	H	E	A			U	K	E		I	D	L	E
			A	C	R	O	B	A	T	I	C			
D	I	A	L		E	W	E			L	A	P	A	Z
A	F	R	I	C	A	N	S	W	A	L	L	O	W	S
M	I	T	Z	I				H	U	B		N	E	A
		D	A	I	L	Y	D	I	G	E	S	T	S	
L	O	E	B		S	A	U	T	E		S	O	O	T
E	C	C	L		A	L	D	E	R		T	O	M	E
O	T	O	E		T	E	E	N	S		S	N	E	E

26

ITEM SPEC PCLAB
ROSY URSA RHONE
AGAR LEAH ELUDE
NOUNIFYINGMOTIF
ACUE LEE
YAM ARRAYED SAG
ABOIL SEA ELIA
WHOLLYTHEMELESS
LONE UKE NIELS
SRS SCORNED KEY
SOC ONOR
JUSTRANDOMWORDS
ECLAT EASE BORE
FLUKE ONES IDEA
FAMED NASH NEWT

27

TGIF RIPE ADAPT
RANI EMIL LONER
ATTN MASH TINNY
MOOGOOGAIPAN
SWERVE ORGANS
RAE DIP SWAP
EGRET RIGID ANA
VOODOOECONOMICS
AFT RUDER TOTEM
DOOM TOY NCR
ERRAND HOOPLA
YOOHOOIMHOME
IDAHO OBIS ISIS
TOTES WISE NEGS
SHAME LETS EROO

28

AUNT BASS YAWNS
SNEE ARLO ETHOS
TRAP ICER SHARE
HERESTHEREMOTE
MABEL TOY SSTS
ALY AHS WEB NUN
EMBED ALERO
ILLMOWTHELAWN
SNAKE SURLY
ISR ROW BAA LBJ
RUGS ROT SPIRE
LETSGOOUTTOEAT
HASAT DARE PSIS
ITSME EDIT UTNE
SEEPS NYSE POST

29

SAFE ADHOC SAGE
CHEX TIARA PURR
AMAH ERROR IDEA
TERIYAKI DENIES
BESS KARAOKE
REGIME CAMEL
AGATE OHNO BEA
JAPANESEIMPORTS
ADE LAWN ELENA
ATOMS BADRAP
IKEBANA SECT
DIALOG PACHINKO
LOGE ANITA MINI
EWES TOTEM ENOL
DART EVADE SEXY

30

LOFTS CAPE BRAG
TULIP ALEX LETO
DRAMA LOCH ALOE
ROCKMUSICIANS
STEREO BARTAB
COD SPASTIC ELY
IOUS GROTTO
PAPERTRAILS
DINEAT DOLL
GAP PRESETS AYE
OROMEO RASPED
SCISSORSKICKS
SAND TOWN HATES
INTO ELIE ETATS
PAYS DOME TERSE

31

A	L	C	O	A		A	E	S	O	P		G	A	S
J	I	H	A	D		D	I	A	N	E		O	N	T
O	V	A	T	E		E	N	R	O	N	L	O	G	O
B	E	N		S	A	L	S			N	I	G	E	L
	B	U	M		L	E	T	T	S		E	L	L	A
T	A	K	E	S	T	H	E	V	A	L	U	E	O	F
R	I	A	T	A			I	A	T	E				
A	T	H	O	U	S	A	N	D	I	N	R	O	M	E
				R	O	L	F			Y	A	H	O	O
S	Y	M	B	O	L	F	O	R	C	A	R	B	O	N
P	E	E	R		D	A	R	E	D		A	O	N	
A	M	N	I	O			M	A	S	K		T	R	U
S	E	T	T	L	E	D	U	P		N	O	H	I	T
M	N	O		E	X	I	L	E		O	B	E	S	E
S	I	R		G	O	M	A	D		T	I	R	E	S

32

R	E	H	A	B		T	O	T	S		T	O	A	D
A	V	I	L	A		R	I	O	T		E	N	D	O
M	A	T	E	Y		A	N	T	I		N	E	M	O
			C	L	O	C	K	O	F	C	H	A	I	R
B	T	U		E	R	E			F	A	U	L	T	S
A	E	N	E	A	S		S	P	E	N	T			
C	A	L	L	F	O	R	C	O	N	E		F	R	I
K	R	I	S			A	O	L			O	R	A	N
S	S	T		C	A	R	T	O	F	C	L	O	V	E
			B	O	N	E	T		R	A	D	N	E	R
S	A	T	U	R	N			C	U	P		T	N	T
C	R	O	C	K	O	F	C	A	G	E	S			
R	I	N	K		Y	E	A	R		C	U	R	I	E
I	S	E	E		E	T	A	L		O	M	I	T	S
P	E	R	T		D	E	N	Y		D	O	D	O	S

33

A	C	M	E		A	E	R		T	S	E	T	S	E
N	O	I	R		J	L	O		O	P	E	R	A	S
D	O	N	A	D	A	M	S		R	O	G	E	R	S
R	E	D	S	O	X		S	P	A	R		A	D	E
E	D	S	E	L		E	I	G	H	T	Y	S	I	X
			S	L	U	R		A	S	Y	O	U		
T	N	T		E	E	N	Y				G	R	I	T
W	O	U	L	D	Y	O	U	B	E	L	I	E	V	E
A	W	R	Y				M	O	N	A		R	Y	E
		B	R	U	S	H		R	O	S	A			
S	H	O	E	P	H	O	N	E		S	N	I	F	F
T	A	J		L	A	N	E		S	O	I	R	E	E
O	N	E	C	A	R		G	E	T	S	M	A	R	T
R	O	T	A	T	E		E	L	O		A	T	M	E
M	I	S	T	E	R		V	F	W		L	E	I	S

34

C	U	R	S		A	M	B	E	R		A	W	A	Y
O	L	E	O		W	I	L	M	A		F	E	T	A
S	C	R	O	L	L	L	O	C	K		F	L	O	W
M	E	A	N	Y		K	N	E	E		A	L	P	S
O	R	N	E	R	Y		D	E	R	A	I	L		
			S	E	E	S				B	R	I	N	E
J	E	S	T		A	P	A	C	H	E		K	E	G
O	N	T		T	R	I	P	L	E	L		E	R	G
L	V	I		A	N	N	E	A	L		O	D	D	S
T	Y	L	E	R				M	E	S	H			
		L	A	P	S	E	S		N	O	M	O	R	E
P	A	L	S		A	S	A	P		I	S	L	A	M
E	X	I	T		S	Q	U	A	L	L	L	I	N	E
R	I	F	E		S	U	N	N	I		A	V	O	N
U	S	E	R		Y	E	A	S	T		W	E	N	D

35

B	R	I	M	S		C	A	I	N		A	R	G	O
R	A	D	I	I		A	C	R	E		V	E	E	R
A	T	E	A	M		B	I	O	S		A	N	T	E
W	I	S	H	I	D	I	D	N	T	K	N	O	W	
N	O	T	A		I	N	S			E	T	U	I	S
			M	U	G	S		A	G	A	I	N	S	T
F	R	U	M	P			A	S	P			C	E	E
L	E	N		N	O	W	W	H	A	T		E	T	A
A	D	D			W	E	S			D	I	D	O	K
T	H	E	W	I	N	D		P	E	S	T			
S	A	R	A	N			S	A	G		S	O	B	S
	I	D	I	D	N	T	K	N	O	W	T	H	E	N
T	R	O	T		E	Y	E	D		I	R	A	T	E
R	E	N	O		A	R	I	A		L	U	R	E	R
A	D	E	N		T	O	N	S		D	E	A	L	T

36

LAPS#LOOSE#HAVE
AREA#OMAHA#ARAL
STAN#RESET#DELI
###DENNISSINNED
OTT#LESS##STATE
DRUMS###CPL#SSS
DANIELNAILED###
SPAN#SANTA#OSLO
###DWAYNEYAWNED
MPG#ETS###INANE
CRAWL##ACID#GAS
GERALDGLARED###
IVAN#ORONO#ALFA
LUGE#PINON#SOIL
LEES#EPEES#HUGE

37

CURTIN##READSTO
OPENBAR#AYKROYD
PIANIST#DECODED
SNL#STERNO#PASS
###REY#EEN#####
JADES#ISR#CHASE
UNIS#ODE#WOEFUL
LIVEFROMNEWYORK
EMEERS#BAT#DOGE
PARDO#MLB#FATES
#####HOE#BEY###
ROTC#ORDEAL#NBC
INERROR#TRIBORO
BELUSHI#HONORER
SIESTAS##NEWMAN

38

LIAR#AMANA#STAN
ACRE#LORES#TOTE
PEOPLEWITHTYPEO
EMU#ORE##YELP##
LASTWORDS#EERIE
SNEER#SEED#DIBS
###AID#BARS#ZIP
#PERSONALITIES#
HEY#EVES#PUG###
AREA#EXES#TOGAS
DUCTS#TREETRUNK
##ACES##AVE#RCA
DONOTWRITERIGHT
ENDS#AOLER#ALOE
FOYT#MOLDY#NERD

39

FRAY#RAIL#RIFTS
YULE#ETRE#EMAIL
ITSA#CLAN#FANNY
#HORSEANDBUGGY#
###NODS##LEE###
GIS#RETRIAL#ASA
ADMIT##IDS#PLUS
MEATANDPOTATOES
MALT#ONE##MAUDE
ALL#GRANITE#DET
###SOS##GONG###
#NICKELANDDIME#
COBRA#AROD#VISE
ADEER#CARL#ESPY
NETWT#EPEE#NONE

40

ERIN#SRTAS#NAME
SOSA#COACH#EVAN
QUITDAYDREAMING
SENHORAS##LEVER
###AGAL#MOMS###
#DONTBESONAIVE#
MENSA##EVE#SEVE
ELI#GETREAL#XER
AVON#GAT##ISERE
#ENOUGHALREADY#
###USSR#AINT###
SLAVE##SOBEREST
COMEDOWNTOEARTH
ALIA#WEISS#PLEA
BLEU#ESTEE#SEMI

41

L	I	M	B		A	T	O	D	D	S		O	S	S
O	N	E	A		C	O	H	E	R	E		D	E	W
B	A	L	C	O	N	Y	S	E	A	T		I	L	E
	S	T	O	V	E			P	B	S		O	L	D
A	L	O	N	E		T	I	L			J	U	T	E
H	U	R		R	A	I	N	Y	S	E	A	S	O	N
A	M	M	O		R	E	V		H	A	P			
	P	E	N	N	Y	S	E	R	E	N	A	D	E	
			E	R	A		R	U	R		N	A	V	E
C	O	M	P	A	N	Y	S	E	A	L		T	A	X
S	C	A	M			E	E	R		I	N	A	P	T
H	U	D		A	B	A			A	D	O	B	E	
A	L	E		M	A	R	K	E	T	S	H	A	R	E
R	A	D		E	L	N	I	N	O		I	S	O	N
P	R	O		R	E	S	T	O	N		T	E	N	T

42

C	L	U	B		S	H	E	L	F		E	L	K	S
L	I	N	E		H	O	M	E	R		L	E	A	K
E	L	I	E		A	L	I	V	E		F	A	Z	E
F	I	T	T	O	B	E	T	I	E	D		S	O	W
			R	U	B	S			P	A	T	H	O	S
C	H	E	E	R	Y		E	R	A	S	E			
H	O	L	D	S		C	R	A	S	H	D	I	E	T
E	P	A			D	O	W	N	S			H	A	H
F	I	N	A	L	E	D	I	T		A	B	O	V	E
			L	I	N	E	N		U	S	O	P	E	N
T	H	R	I	F	T			O	S	H	A			
A	A	A		T	U	R	N	T	H	E	T	I	D	E
G	I	Z	A		R	O	U	T	E		M	A	I	D
U	K	E	S		E	L	D	E	R		A	G	E	D
P	U	S	H		S	E	E	R	S		N	O	S	Y

43

S	A	T		K	R	I	L	L		T	I	L	T	S
P	E	R		I	N	D	I	A		I	C	A	H	N
I	R	E		L	A	S	T	S	A	M	U	R	A	I
E	I	E	I	O			H	E	R	B		A	N	T
L	E	S	T	W	E	F	O	R	G	E	T			
			S	A	B	E			O	R	A	N	G	E
C	H	A		T	R	A	I	T			C	O	E	D
L	I	S	T	T	O	S	T	A	R	B	O	A	R	D
A	R	I	A			T	O	N	E	R		H	E	Y
D	E	S	I	R	E			T	A	U	S			
			L	O	S	T	H	E	R	S	H	E	E	P
S	T	A		O	S	H	A			S	A	R	G	E
L	U	S	T	F	O	R	L	I	F	E		O	R	E
A	B	A	S	E		E	A	S	E	L		D	E	L
P	A	P	E	R		E	S	T	E	S		E	T	S

44

N	A	P	A		A	P	S	E	S			O	F	F
I	C	E	S		B	O	O	N	S		A	P	I	E
C	H	E	S	T	S	O	F	D	R	A	W	E	R	S
E	E	L		H	O	R	A	S		F	A	C	E	T
			T	A	R				A	O	L			
L	I	G	H	T	B	U	L	B	J	O	K	E		
I	D	L	E	S		R	U	R	A	L		F	R	O
S	E	E	M		S	I	L	E	X		B	R	A	M
T	E	A		S	E	A	L	S		S	I	E	G	E
		M	A	T	C	H	S	T	I	C	K	M	E	N
			G	A	T				G	R	E			
S	C	A	N	T		D	R	A	N	O		U	S	A
T	H	R	E	E	P	R	E	S	I	D	E	N	T	S
E	A	T	S		S	A	D	A	T		R	I	O	T
M	R	S			S	T	O	N	E		E	X	P	O

45

H	A	N	G		E	P	S	O	M		I	H	O	P
O	N	E	A		P	O	P	P	A		G	U	L	L
S	T	A	R		I	C	E	I	N		U	R	G	E
S	I	T	B	A	C	K	A	N	D	R	E	L	A	X
			L	P	S		K	E	Y	E	S			
M	I	M	E	O		P	O	D		L	S	A	T	S
E	W	E			R	E	F		M	I	S	C	U	E
D	O	W	N	F	O	R	T	H	E	C	O	U	N	T
I	N	L	A	I	D		H	A	G			R	E	A
A	T	S	I	X		R	E	D		B	L	A	S	T
			L	I	M	E	D		O	O	O			
C	O	M	E	T	O	T	E	R	M	S	W	I	T	H
A	X	E	D		L	I	V	E	N		E	D	A	M
S	E	M	I		T	R	I	N	I		N	I	N	O
K	N	O	T		S	E	L	E	S		D	O	G	S

46

L	E	N	O		D	F	L	A	T		A	S	T	I
E	V	I	L		A	R	O	M	A		M	E	I	R
S	A	G	E		M	E	T	E	R		B	R	A	E
		H	O	U	S	E	T	R	A	I	L	E	R	S
A	C	T		R	E	O				M	E	N	A	T
F	A	C	I	A	L	F	E	A	T	U	R	E	S	
A	T	A	L	L			R	U	B	S				
R	O	P	E		P	A	R	K	S		A	T	R	A
				E	A	S	E			S	T	R	E	P
	C	A	R	T	R	I	D	G	E	C	L	I	P	S
T	R	E	A	T				O	V	A		E	S	O
B	E	R	M	U	D	A	S	H	O	R	T	S		
S	W	A	M		E	B	O	O	K		O	O	P	S
P	E	T	E		F	L	U	M	E		G	U	R	U
S	L	E	D		T	Y	P	E	D		A	T	O	P

47

A	R	I	S	E		R	A	B	B	I		B	A	T
L	U	N	A	R		A	L	L	A	N		A	R	E
V	E	I	L	O	F	T	I	E	R	S		B	E	E
A	S	T	U	T	E		T	A	R		R	Y	A	N
			D	I	V	A		T	I	N	E	S		
A	L	S		C	E	N	T	S	O	F	S	I	T	E
L	A	M	S		R	N	A			L	I	T	E	R
G	N	A	T		S	A	U	N	A		S	T	A	N
E	A	T	E	N			P	A	N		T	E	S	S
R	I	T	E	O	F	W	E	I	G	H		R	E	T
		E	R	R	O	R		L	E	E	R			
M	A	R	S		R	E	A		L	I	A	B	L	E
U	R	I		P	E	A	C	E	O	F	M	E	E	T
T	I	N		A	S	T	H	E		E	I	E	I	O
T	A	G		O	T	H	E	R		R	E	R	A	N

48

S	P	A	T		S	A	I	L		M	I	R	E	D
I	O	T	A		E	B	R	O		Y	O	U	R	E
N	U	T	C	R	A	C	K	E	R	S	U	I	T	E
A	N	Y	H	O	W		S	W	A	T		N	E	D
I	D	S		W	A	C		S	P	I	T			
			A	S	T	R	O		S	Q	U	A	T	S
A	M	A	T		E	E	L	S		U	R	I	A	H
B	O	L	T	F	R	O	M	T	H	E	B	L	U	E
R	A	T	I	O		N	O	R	A		A	S	T	A
A	T	O	L	L	S		S	A	T	I	N			
			A	L	A	S		Y	R	S		A	C	C
A	S	A		O	A	T	S		A	N	I	M	A	L
S	C	R	E	W	B	A	L	L	C	O	M	E	D	Y
P	A	N	A	M		R	O	O	K		A	B	E	D
S	N	O	R	E		E	G	O	S		M	A	T	E

49

S	U	M	A	C	S		C	B	S		S	T	A	T
A	T	O	N	A	L		O	L	E		L	E	A	R
W	I	N	D	T	U	N	N	E	L		E	S	A	U
I	C	E	R		S	E	A	N		S	E	T		
N	A	T	E		H	A	N	D	P	U	P	P	E	T
			T	R	Y				U	P	S	I	Z	E
A	G	A	T	E		G	R	A	S	P		L	I	N
F	I	N	I	S	H	I	N	G	S	E	C	O	N	D
R	A	T		P	A	S	S	E		R	O	T	E	S
O	N	E	T	O	N				E	S	P			
S	T	R	I	N	G	B	E	A	N		A	D	A	M
		O	D	D		L	A	R	D		P	E	L	E
B	L	O	B		B	E	S	T	S	E	L	L	E	R
M	I	M	I		R	A	Y		U	S	E	F	U	L
W	E	S	T		A	K	A		P	L	A	T	T	E

50

J	I	V	E		A	S	A	B	C		W	I	T	S
O	T	O	E		L	O	Y	A	L		O	R	A	N
C	O	U	N	T	B	A	S	I	E		O	I	S	E
K	O	S		R	U	R		L	A	R	D	N	E	R
			C	O	M		B	O	N	E	Y	A	R	D
A	T	B	A	T		H	I	R	S	C	H			
G	A	R	B		T	U	G		E	D	E	R	L	E
O	T	I	C		U	N	B	A	R		R	O	A	D
B	A	T	A	A	N		A	R	S		M	A	N	Y
			L	E	A	R	N	T		D	A	N	E	S
S	L	A	L	O	M	E	D		M	E	N			
W	A	G	O	N	E	R		L	I	P		T	A	J
I	S	A	W		L	O	U	I	S	P	R	I	M	A
N	E	V	A		T	O	G	A	S		I	N	E	Z
G	R	E	Y		S	T	O	R	M		B	E	N	Z

51

AGOG UPSET NEWT
LOBE GOTTI ISEE
PROATHLETE GAPE
OPERA SMASHHITS
URL OUT
SUPPORTINGCAST
SHH SCORN SANTA
AAHS HOUND PIED
AMUCK STIES SEA
BEHINDTHEWHEEL
SIR YON
CABSTANDS VALUE
OSLO FORTHEBEST
STIR TONER LENA
TOPS SNOWS ERAS

52

FLO LEAR REDCAP
LOU ORNE INARUT
OCT CLEF NOMADS
PAPAHEMINGWAY
PLUMS ILE TOFU
YETI MAMALEONES
STA STAN ETE
BASSIST ONORDER
OHO POOH ESO
BABYSNOOKS GUST
OSSA TRE OUNCE
THETHREEBEARS
SHOOTS ONME BET
AURORA REMY LEE
GEYSER SRAS END

53

IMAGE ETNA PAPA
RANON AGIN ABET
ACCOUNTING RUST
DRU FORTASTE
SALIENT YODELS
SPUDS HAT RESET
SOLE BANANA
PLACELIKEHOME
RAISED NEMO
AMUSE AER STRIP
SATEEN SOTHERE
TIMELIKE ARE
ETON THEPRESENT
RASA RANI ALCOA
NITS ONYX KYOTO

54

PANG DEBT CHIME
OBOE ELIE RIDER
KILT ALLS ALERT
EDAM FALLINLOVE
RENAME SAVE
RAND ASSISI
SNARL OMAN EDEN
LIMIT POP STEAD
ALIE DEMS ITALY
MEDDLE EARL
ANTI DEEPER
GETENGAGED DASH
ILIAD LIVE OTTO
RINSE OVEN WIEN
LATER NERD NOSE

55

HOBBY MARC STAG
OPERA OLEO HERR
TADAS JOAN ANNE
HOWSHOULDIKNOW
FLEE MODE
SLR RAMP STIFLE
WOOS DOIN ATRIA
ITSANYONESGUESS
STEVE DECK PELE
HOSERS SKID FED
STEM EURO
CANTSAYFORSURE
AUDI LEAP TBALL
PRAM EYRE ELLIS
SAKE DEED DELED

56

J	E	S	T		A	T	I	T		D	R	A	B	S
U	N	T	O		B	A	C	H		Y	O	W	I	E
D	R	A	W	P	O	K	E	R		E	T	H	A	N
G	O	N	N	A		E	D	E	N			I	S	T
E	N	D		C	B	S		S	Y	B	I	L		
			S	K	E	T	C	H	C	O	M	E	D	Y
	B	O	O	S	T	E	R			O	P	A	R	T
S	O	U	L		S	N	I	T	S		A	G	E	D
I	O	T	A	S			M	I	L	K	C	O	W	
T	R	A	C	E	E	L	E	M	E	N	T			
		N	E	A	T	O		E	W	E		S	A	G
S	A	D			A	N	E	W		L	A	T	H	E
A	V	O	W	S		D	R	A	F	T	B	E	E	R
R	O	U	E	N		O	G	R	E		B	E	A	M
I	N	T	E	L		N	O	P	E		E	D	D	Y

57

G	R	A	S	P		S	A	C	S		I	M	S	O
R	I	G	O	R		O	M	O	O		N	O	O	K
A	B	E	L	I	N	C	O	L	N		L	O	B	S
S	E	N	I	O	R	C	I	T	I	Z	E	N	S	
S	Y	D		R	A	E			A	S	T	U	T	E
Y	E	A	R			R	A	M		A	S	N	O	T
			E	O	N		D	I	T	Z		I	R	S
	J	U	N	I	O	R	V	A	R	S	I	T	Y	
T	A	R		L	I	L	I		I	A	N			
O	N	E	A	L		S	L	R			E	S	P	Y
N	I	T	R	I	C			E	L	K		T	O	V
	T	H	E	T	H	I	R	D	E	S	T	A	T	E
R	O	A	N		I	N	C	O	N	T	E	M	P	T
D	R	N	O		P	L	A	N		A	T	E	I	T
A	S	E	T		S	A	S	E		R	E	N	E	E

58

A	S	H	C	A	N		S	H	U	T		E	S	Q
C	L	A	U	D	E		M	A	H	I		T	H	U
R	U	N	J	E	S	S	E	R	U	N		H	O	I
E	R	G	O		S	Y	L	P	H		B	A	E	Z
				J	I	L	L	S		R	O	N		
E	M	A	N	U	E	L			R	E	X	A	L	L
M	U	L	A	N		A	O	R	T	A		L	E	O
B	L	O	W	G	A	B	R	I	E	L	B	L	O	W
E	T	H		L	A	I	R	S		I	R	E	N	E
D	I	A	L	E	R			O	C	T	A	N	E	S
		S	I	S		R	E	T	R	Y				
H	D	T	V		S	O	R	T	A		O	A	S	T
I	D	A		F	L	Y	R	O	B	I	N	F	L	Y
V	A	T		Y	O	K	O		B	A	Z	A	A	R
E	Y	E		I	G	O	R		E	M	E	R	G	E

59

K	C	A	R		A	T	S	E	A		C	A	D	S
E	U	R	O		T	R	E	V	I		A	B	E	L
G	R	I	M	R	E	A	P	E	R		J	O	E	Y
			P	E	S	C	I			M	O	I	R	E
C	C	S		S	T	E	A	M	R	O	L	L	E	R
H	E	I	S	T	S			A	O	N	E			
A	L	S	O			S	T	Y	L	E		B	S	S
M	I	S	T	E	R	I	N	B	E	T	W	E	E	N
P	A	Y		M	A	T	T	E			A	N	N	O
			S	I	Z	E			O	D	D	J	O	B
F	I	R	M	R	E	S	O	L	V	E		I	R	S
A	R	I	E	S			G	E	E	S	E			
L	A	V	A		W	O	R	M	R	I	D	D	E	N
S	T	A	R		E	L	E	M	I		G	U	R	U
E	E	L	S		B	E	S	E	T		E	D	E	N

60

H	A	R	S	H		I	C	A	N		L	O	L	A
A	L	I	C	E		N	A	T	O		I	B	I	S
N	A	D	I	R		C	R	O	C		N	O	A	H
G	R	E	E	N	B	A	Y	P	A	C	K	E	R	
	M	A	N	I	A				R	I	A			
			C	A	R	P	E	T	B	A	G	G	E	R
M	I	L	E		T	E	X	A	S		E	L	L	E
E	T	A				T	U	N				U	S	A
S	E	M	I		M	E	R	G	E		D	E	E	M
A	M	A	T	E	U	R	B	O	X	E	R			
			A	T	T				E	G	E	S	T	
	V	O	L	C	A	N	I	C	C	R	A	T	E	R
M	A	G	I		N	O	V	A		E	M	O	T	E
O	L	L	A		T	S	A	R		T	O	R	R	E
P	E	E	N		S	Y	N	E		S	N	E	A	K

61

H	A	R	P		P	L	A	N		P	A	D	R	E
O	L	E	O		R	O	M	A		O	B	O	E	S
B	E	F	O	R	E	Y	O	U	K	N	O	W	I	T
B	U	R	L	A	P		I	S	I	T		N	N	E
S	T	Y		G	P	S		E	D	I	T	S		
			Q	U	I	C	K	A	S	A	W	I	N	K
	M	S	U		N	A	M			C	O	Z	E	N
R	O	T	I		G	R	A	B	S		B	E	R	T
B	E	E	C	H			R	A	P		I	D	O	
I	N	A	H	E	A	R	T	B	E	A	T			
		D	E	R	M	A		E	E	G		A	B	C
A	L	Y		B	A	T	S		D	E	A	R	I	E
R	I	G	H	T	T	H	I	S	S	E	C	O	N	D
C	L	I	M	E		E	T	T	U		R	A	G	E
S	I	G	M	A		R	E	A	P		E	R	O	S

62

T	A	M	P	A		S	A	P	S		C	H	A	T
E	M	A	I	L		L	I	E	N		O	I	L	Y
N	O	N	C	E		I	M	D	O	I	N	G	O	K
T	R	E	K		S	P	E	D		T	E	H	E	E
H	E	S	A	R	E	B	E	L		E	S	P		
			P	O	N	Y		I	S	M		O	S	S
S	C	R	A	P	S		G	N	U		B	I	L	E
Y	O	U	R	E	A	B	I	G	B	O	Y	N	O	W
S	E	N	T		T	O	N		S	K	A	T	E	S
T	N	T		S	E	X		S	I	L	L			
		O	O	P		S	H	E	S	A	L	A	D	Y
S	A	S	H	A		C	A	T	T		O	B	I	E
T	H	E	Y	R	E	O	F	F		E	D	I	N	A
I	S	E	E		E	R	T	E		A	D	D	E	R
R	O	D	S		L	E	S	E		U	S	E	R	S

63

S	T	U	T	Z		I	M	A	M		P	A	V	E
P	O	L	E	S		G	I	N	O		U	S	E	R
O	N	C	E	A	M	O	N	T	H		R	H	E	A
I	K	E		Z	E	R	O		A	L	P	E	R	T
L	A	R	O	S	A		T	R	I	A	L			
			R	A	G	A		O	R	D	E	A	L	S
I	R	M	A		E	G	G	O		S	H	R	E	K
M	O	A	N		R	H	Y	M	E		E	B	A	Y
A	M	I	G	O		A	M	E	X		A	S	K	S
C	A	M	E	R	A	S		R	O	A	R			
			J	E	S	T	S		D	I	T	T	O	S
T	H	R	U	S	T		P	L	U	M		A	B	O
M	A	U	I		H	I	Y	O	S	I	L	V	E	R
A	L	E	C		M	O	O	G		N	O	I	S	E
N	O	S	E		A	N	N	E		G	A	S	E	S

64

S	M	O	G		S	T	A	G	E		M	E	S	A
L	A	V	A		H	O	V	E	R		U	S	P	S
A	X	E	R		O	R	I	O	N		E	S	A	U
G	I	N	G	E	R	R	O	G	E	R	S			
			O	F	T	E	N			A	L	P	E	N
P	A	P	Y	R	U	S		G	A	L	I	L	E	O
A	M	I	L	E			O	M	S			A	L	T
R	O	S	E	M	A	R	Y	C	L	O	O	N	E	Y
R	E	C			N	F	L			S	P	A	R	E
O	B	E	L	I	S	K		A	M	H	E	R	S	T
T	A	S	E	R			G	O	R	E	N			
			P	E	P	P	E	R	M	A	R	T	I	N
B	O	D	E		A	I	R	T	O		O	U	Z	O
M	U	I	R		S	T	R	A	T		A	T	O	P
W	I	N	S		S	A	Y	S	O		D	U	D	E

65

U	N	R	I	P		A	P	E	D		H	I	R	E
S	A	E	N	S		R	U	R	A	L	A	R	E	A
S	K	A	T	I	N	G	M	A	N	E	U	V	E	R
R	E	S			O	O	P	S		A	L	I	V	E
	D	O	W	N	O	N			E	V	E	N	E	D
A	M	N	I	O	N		S	T	E	E	R			
G	A	E	L	S		C	O	I	L			C	U	E
R	J	R	E	Y	N	O	L	D	S	B	R	A	N	D
O	A	S			E	N	V	Y		L	A	N	C	E
			A	T	O	N	E		W	A	N	T	O	N
W	O	O	D	E	N			P	I	S	T	O	L	
A	S	P	E	N		E	A	R	L			N	O	S
S	H	I	P	O	F	T	H	E	D	E	S	E	R	T
N	E	U	T	R	I	N	O	S		M	O	S	E	Y
T	A	M	S		B	A	T	S		S	W	E	D	E

66

C	A	D	G	E		D	E	A	N		A	R	C	H
A	C	O	R	N		R	E	N	O		L	U	A	U
G	R	E	A	T		E	R	O	S		I	N	C	A
Y	E	S	V	I	R	G	I	N	I	A		I	A	N
			E	R	A	S	E		E	G	G	N	O	G
T	I	N	S	E	L			D	R	N	O			
R	O	O	T		P	L	I	E		E	B	B	E	D
I	T	I		T	H	E	R	E	I	S		A	A	R
P	A	R	S	E		A	E	R	O		A	L	V	A
			A	S	A	P			N	U	T	M	E	G
C	A	R	O	L	S		S	E	I	N	E			
A	B	A		A	S	A	N	T	A	C	L	A	U	S
D	I	V	A		U	H	O	H		L	I	L	L	E
I	T	E	M		M	O	R	E		A	E	T	N	A
Z	E	N	O		E	Y	E	R		D	R	E	A	M

67

H	E	E	L		F	I	E	F		H	A	M	E	L
A	L	A	I		O	N	T	O		A	M	U	L	E
H	M	S	B	O	U	N	T	Y		S	O	F	I	A
A	S	T	R	A	L		A	T	T	H	E	T	O	P
			E	R	S	T			H	A	B	I	T	S
D	O	L	T	S		E	S	P	A	N	A			
A	L	I	T		P	A	P	A	Y	A		F	U	R
F	A	M	O	U	S	R	A	C	E	H	O	R	S	E
T	V	A		N	E	A	R	E	R		N	A	M	E
			N	E	U	T	E	R		P	E	N	A	L
E	N	N	E	A	D			S	E	R	F			
M	A	I	L	R	O	O	M		L	A	I	D	U	P
I	D	E	S	T		J	E	L	L	Y	F	I	S	H
R	I	C	O	H		A	L	O	E		T	R	E	Y
S	A	E	N	S		I	S	B	N		H	E	R	S

68

M	A	R	A	T		C	A	R	O	M		A	T	M
A	T	A	R	I		A	R	O	A	R		R	O	I
C	O	M	I	C	A	C	T	O	R	S		M	O	M
R	O	I	L		L	A	O	S		C	C	C	L	I
O	T	S		S	M	O	O	T		R	A	H		
			T	O	A				C	A	M	A	R	O
A	S	S	O	C		I	M	H	O	T		I	O	S
A	C	H	R	I	S	T	M	A	S	C	A	R	O	L
H	O	I		A	T	O	M	S		H	A	S	T	O
S	T	R	O	L	L				A	I	R			
		T	L	C		S	H	A	L	T		C	A	L
T	O	T	A	L		M	A	S	T		C	A	L	I
A	R	A		A	L	A	S	T	A	I	R	S	I	M
T	A	I		S	O	L	T	I		M	A	C	A	O
A	L	L		S	O	L	A	R		A	M	A	S	S

69

B	A	R		A	E	T	N	A		D	E	G	A	S
A	T	O		S	Q	U	A	T		E	N	O	L	A
S	O	B		P	U	L	P	F	I	C	T	I	O	N
S	P	E	C	I	A	L			D	A	R	N	E	D
		R	U	N	T		T	E	L	L	Y			
M	A	T	T		O	Z	O	N	E		F	E	S	T
A	L	P		T	R	A	P	S		S	E	A	T	O
T	E	E	T	H		P	S	I		R	E	S	I	N
E	V	E	R	Y		A	E	G	I	S		T	N	T
S	E	L	A		S	T	E	N	S		L	O	G	O
			S	T	E	A	D		O	M	A	R		
A	R	C	H	I	E			S	T	E	W	A	R	D
J	U	I	C	E	N	E	W	T	O	N		N	O	R
A	L	T	A	R		S	H	O	P	S		G	T	O
R	E	I	N	S		T	Y	P	E	A		E	S	P

70

M	A	G	I		T	E	L	L		A	R	M	O	R
A	M	E	N		E	X	I	T		D	O	O	N	E
J	O	E	J	E	T	T	E	R		L	O	T	S	A
			A	F	R	O	S		D	I	T	H	E	R
A	D	M	I	R	A	L		S	O	B		E	T	S
D	O	Y	L	E			C	E	N	S	O	R		
O	R	S		M	I	N	U	E	T		A	J	A	R
B	A	T	S		S	O	F	T	G		F	U	S	E
E	L	E	C		O	N	F	O	O	T		I	S	A
		R	I	F	L	E	S			A	R	C	E	D
B	E	Y		A	D	S		A	N	X	I	E	T	Y
I	N	J	O	K	E		T	R	E	E	S			
B	R	E	V	E		J	U	N	E	S	Q	U	A	D
L	O	S	E	R		A	T	A	D		U	R	G	E
E	N	T	R	Y		S	U	Z	Y		E	L	A	N

71

72

ALEC SPEED BAAL
MIDI PRUDE ARNO
PEER HORAS NATO
UNCLETOMSCABIN
LIRE EON
IREMEMBERMAMA
SNARE LITE ORE
ISIS SPINS PURE
PUN STAN FERAL
MYCOUSINVINNY
LON OILS
ALLINTHEFAMILY
PAIN CALEB OYEZ
STAG ARIEL NOTA
OHMY REESE SNIP

73

LORD JEAN SCHMO
OPUS ABLE CHURN
WHITESALE ROSIE
MEN ROY SLEPT
ALISON COLESLAW
SINUS CONAN EYE
SAGS PAN MESSES
HEADSTART
LARIAT IRS OAKS
ABE TANGY AMPLE
BUCKSKIN TIPPER
ANAIS KIM REP
ALLOW SANDSTONE
DELTA ALOE OVEN
SISSY NIBS TEXT

74

75